HOW TO CREATE
THE NEXT FACEBOOK

SEEING YOUR STARTUP THROUGH,
FROM IDEA TO IPO

Tom Taulli

How to Create the Next Facebook: Seeing Your Startup Through, from Idea to IPO

ISBN-13 (pbk): 978-1-4302-4647-3
ISBN-13 (electronic): 978-1-4302-4648-0

Trademarked names may appear in this book. Rather than use a trademark symbol with every occurrence of a trademarked name, we use the names only in an editorial fashion and to the benefit of the trademark owner, with no intention of infringement of the trademark.

President and Publisher: Paul Manning
Lead Editor: Morgan Ertel
Editorial Board: Steve Anglin, Mark Beckner, Ewan Buckingham, Gary Cornell, Louise Corrigan, Morgan Ertel, Jonathan Gennick, Jonathan Hassell, Robert Hutchinson, Michelle Lowman, James Markham, Matthew Moodie, Jeff Olson, Jeffrey Pepper, Douglas Pundick, Ben Renow-Clarke, Dominic Shakeshaft, Gwenan Spearing, Matt Wade, Tom Welsh
Coordinating Editor: Rita Fernando
Copy Editor: Tiffany Taylor and Catherine Ohala
Compositor: Bytheway Publishing Services
Indexer: SPi Global
Cover Designer: Anna Ishchenko

Distributed to the book trade worldwide by Springer-Verlag New York, Inc., 233 Spring Street, 6th Floor, New York, NY 10013. Phone 1-800-SPRINGER, fax 201-348-4505, e-mail orders-ny@springer-sbm.com, or visit www.springeronline.com.

For information on translations, please contact us by e-mail at info@apress.com, or visit www.apress.com.

Apress and friends of ED books may be purchased in bulk for academic, corporate, or promotional use. eBook versions and licenses are also available for most titles. For more information, reference our Special Bulk Sales–eBook Licensing web page at www.apress.com/bulk-sales. To place an order, email your request to support@apress.com

Contents

Foreword

Being an entrepreneur is hard. It's a roller coaster every day. You need a strong stomach, eyes on the future, a soul that wants to change the world, and a heart that believes you can do it. You learn, you fail, you learn some more. The Internet landscape has changed a lot since I started my first company in 1999. Since Facebook launched, we've all been pushed to step up our game. There's been a shift in the technology field to move faster than ever before, while creating value for your users.

"Move fast and break things." "Done is better than perfect." Before these clichéd mantras made their way into mainstream startup culture, they described a simple Facebook philosophy—to ship code fast and continuously iterate. Although we've always moved pretty quickly in Silicon Valley, Facebook has driven us to move even quicker. At BranchOut, we're pushed to keep up with Facebook's weekly development cycles because we're an application built on their platform. We've embraced the developer-driven culture behind the "move fast" mentality because the faster we ship code, the quicker we can make mistakes and learn from them.

There are a lot of competing interests at play when you're building a company. Facebook had a lot of interest early on in diverging from the path they were on. In 2004, Friendster attempted to acquire Facebook for $10 million. Had that happened, who knows if Facebook would have added photo sharing the next year, eventually opened up to anyone with an e-mail address, and ultimately made the world as open and connected as it is today? When you're building a company, there's a lot of outside pressure to hit particular metrics and deadlines. You get a lot of advice. But it all comes down to listening to your users. If you don't build a passionate company, they won't come back. At BranchOut, we're trying to make our users' lives better. We're trying to help people represent themselves professionally so they can network, find mentors, and land their dream jobs.

Create value. Run fast, go big, and change the world.

Rick Marini
Founder of BranchOut

About the Author

Tom Taulli is based in Silicon Valley, in the heart of IPO land. On a regular basis, he talks with many of the top tech CEOs and founders to find the next hot deals and discover which startups are stinkers. A long-time follower of the IPO scene, Taulli started one of the first sites in the space, called WebIPO, in the mid-1990s. It was a place where investors obtained research as well as access to deals for the dot-com boom. From there, he started several other companies, such as  Hypermart.net, which was sold to InfoSpace in 1999. Currently, Taulli is an advisor to tech companies and writes extensively on tech, finance, and IPOs. His work has appeared on Forbes.com, TechWeb, and *BusinessWeek*. He is also frequently quoted in publications like the *Wall Street Journal* and is regularly interviewed on CNBC and BloombergTV. You can follow him on Twitter at @ttaulli.

Introduction

OK, the title of this book is definitely provocative. Who wouldn't want to create the next Facebook and become extremely wealthy and famous? No doubt, the company's success has inspired many people to become entrepreneurs. It has become the hot thing nowadays.

But my book is not about replicating Facebook. After all, the company has become the mega winner in social networking. History has shown that when critical mass is established in a new market, the leader usually keeps its position for many years. Just look at Google, Microsoft, Skype, and eBay.

Achieving dominance is often a matter of a few key decisions. Companies like MySpace and Friendster could easily have become the leader. Hey, my book might have been called *How to Create the Next MySpace* or *How to Create the Next Friendster* if history had been different.

The goal of this book is to look at the critical aspects of how Facebook went from $0 to over $50 billion in 8 years. But I don't just cover the success; I also look at the mistakes. Some were almost fatal.

Here's a rundown of the book's main areas:

Chapter 1—"The Mission": Your mission should be a huge goal. You want to change the world in some way, and this is a powerful driver for success. It gets employees excited as well as investors and customers.

Chapter 2—"Legal": This stuff is boring and tedious but critically important. In the early days, Mark Zuckerberg nearly destroyed his company as a result of bad legal decisions.

Chapter 3—"The Product": Zuckerberg is a product genius. But to be successful, you don't have to be a natural-born prodigy. This chapter looks at best practices to make products that customers love.

Chapters 4, 5, and 6—"Raising Capital," "The Pitch," and "Deal Terms": Here's everything you need to know to get investors to write checks. Even highly successful companies need to raise money—and Facebook has been fundraising from the start. In its history, the company has raised more than $18 billion.

Chapter 7—"Go-To-Market": This topic gets little attention from entrepreneurs, and it's a big oversight. If you don't have a solid go-to-market strategy, your venture will probably fail.

Chapter 8—"The Financials": This is another boring topic (sorry!). But don't skip it. Although the tech industry goes through periods where fundamentals don't seem to matter much, they are temporary manias. In the end, you need to understand the nuts and bolts of a company's financials.

Chapter 9—"The Business Model": This is how your company makes money. Chances are, you have one core revenue stream. This chapter looks at some of the main business models that have worked.

Chapter 10—"Being a Great CEO": Zuckerberg was not a natural-born CEO. In fact, he was terrible at the role, at least during the first couple of years of Facebook's history. But he was determined to get better. Being a CEO is definitely something that can be learned.

Chapter 11—"The Team": Zuckerberg has always understood the importance of creating a cohesive team. But he also realizes that there are times when people need to be let go.

Chapter 12—"M&A": Since 2007, Zuckerberg has struck over 25 acquisitions. Most were ways to get talent, a process known as an acqui-hire. This chapter explains how to bolster your company with deal-making.

Chapter 13—"Selling Your Company": Zuckerberg is focused on keeping his company independent. But the fact is, most companies are eventually sold off. This chapter looks at how to maximize the value of a transaction.

Chapter 14—"IPO": In 2012, Facebook came public. Yes, it was a challenging deal, but the company had the second largest transaction in US history. This chapter shows what it takes to go public.

Chapter 15—"Wealth Management": As an entrepreneur, you have the opportunity to get rich. However, you need to make sure you manage your wealth properly. There are many horror stories about entrepreneurs who have lost fortunes.

Chapter 16—"Conclusion": In this chapter, I look at some takeaways and big opportunities for you to think about.

Why should I be the person to write this book? Well, I do have a unique perspective. I have started several companies in tech and have raised capital from angels and venture capitalists. I also sold one of my companies to a public company. At the same time, I've made angel investments and have advised companies.

All of these experiences have been extremely valuable. In this book, I try to bring out these lessons. I wish I had known these things when I started my first business!

For the past 15 years, I have also been a writer. I have written 10 books on finance and technology. I have also written for publications like *BusinessWeek* and *Forbes*. In the process, I have talked to many great entrepreneurs, such as Google's Sergey Brin and Twitter's Evan Williams. It has been a great learning experience.

Enough with the intro. Let's get started!

The Mission

The revolution is not an apple that falls when it is ripe. You have to make it fall.

—Che Guevara

If you go to Mark Zuckerberg's Facebook page, you'll see that it says: "I'm trying to make the world a more open place."[1] It's a grand mission for any person. But, of course, it is essentially the mission of his company. In Zuckerberg's letter to shareholders in Facebook's initial public offering (IPO) prospectus, he says: "Facebook was not originally created to be a company. It was built to accomplish a social mission—to make the world more open and connected."[2] This is not the kind of mission you often associate with a company, but all great companies are about a cosmic vision, and that vision is always based on the power of a founder like Howard Schultz, Walt Disney, Henry Ford, Steve Jobs, and Bill Gates. They are more than just chief executive officers (CEOs). They are revolutionaries.

Every day, Facebook affects the lives of millions of people. It helps make friendships strong and even leads to marriages. Facebook makes it possible to understand different cultures and ideas. In some cases, its impact can be game changing. Facebook is an essential communication tool in times of disaster, such as when the horrendous tsunami hit Japan in March 2011. It can even lead to radical changes in societies, as seen with the Arab Spring.

In Facebook's IPO prospectus, Zuckerberg wrote:

> By giving people the power to share, we are starting to see people make their voices heard on a different scale from what has historically been possible. These voices will increase in number and volume. They cannot be ignored. Over

[1] www.facebook.com/pages/Mark-Zukerberg/156559947734345
[2] "Facebook IPO Prospectus," May 17, 2012, www.sec.gov/Archives/edgar/data/1326801/000119312512240111/d287954d424b4.htm

*time, we expect governments will become more responsive to issues and
concerns raised directly by all their people rather than through intermediaries
controlled by a select few.[3]*

Now, it is true that, despite its mission, Facebook is no utopian paradise.
Change can get messy. Facebook can actually destroy friendships or lead to
bullying or divorce. It is a place where mean, terrible things happen. Yet on the
whole, Facebook has been a positive force in the lives of countless people
around the world. Why else would more than 500 million people visit the site
every day?

The popularity and empowering nature of Facebook has turned Zuckerberg
into one of the towering figures of his generation. Besides being one of the
richest people on Earth, he has many other notable accomplishments, such as
being selected as *Time Magazine*'s Person of the Year in 2010. He even got to
meet the president. All of this and Zuckerberg is only 28 years old.

But it all started with a mission—something that resonates with everyone on
Earth—and that's a big lesson for entrepreneurs. You need to create something
worth working for. You must want to wake up every morning with a sole and
abiding obsession with your mission. The mission will drive your employees,
it will get your customers excited, it may even change the world.

Zuckerberg's mission was not necessarily original. In fact, the concept of
a social network had many historical precedents, the first of which—the
telegraph—sent electronic messages across wires and required the knowledge
of a special language called *Morse code*. The mastermind of this technology
was Samuel Morse. While attending Yale in 1808, Morse became interested in
the concept and uses of electricity. Then, in 1832, Morse took a voyage that
would change his life and the course of history. On this trip, he met Charles
Thomas Jackson, an expert in electromagnetism, who showed Morse several
experiments with his electromagnet. It was then, after he began to understand
the physics of electromagnetism, that Morse started to develop the idea of a
telegraph, which would use electromagnetism to send messages across long
distances using cheap, low-quality wire. There were several other inventors
who had the same idea at the time, but Morse had more financial resources
and was quicker than the others to share his invention. Morse launched the
telegraph in Morristown, New Jersey, in 1838, and the technology spread
quickly. It even led to the creation of a fast-growing communications
business—Western Union.

The telegraph was only the jumping off point in the history of social networking.
In 1876, Alexander Graham Bell invented the telephone. As was the case with
the telegraph, there was someone else, Elisha Gray, who had the same idea at

[3] Ibid.

the same time. However, Bell got to the patent office first—by only a few hours—which demonstrates that speed is always crucial in technology!

Zuckerberg had the same kind of experiences with Facebook. There were other sites, like Friendster and MySpace, that were also based on the same concept of an online social network. But Zuckerberg did things better and faster. Is it any wonder that one of his favorite songs is Punk Daft's "Harder Better Faster"?

As is the case with all great new technologies, Facebook had many doubters. It's natural for critics to doubt anything that is truly innovative. When Western Union evaluated the telephone, its conclusion was: "It has too many shortcomings to be seriously considered as a means of communication. The device is inherently of no value to us."[4] With regard to Facebook, critics doubted that people would put all their personal information on a web site. But when Zuckerberg launched Facebook, he was convinced of his mission and that Facebook would be the best way to pursue it.

Facebook is not alone in the determined way it seeks to fulfill its mission. All of today's successful companies—companies of all kinds and in all industries— similarly air their commitments to the world and then strive, day in and day out, to keep them. Table 1-1 contains the mission statements of just a handful of today's most successful companies.

Table 1-1. Mission Statements from Current Successful Companies

Company	Mission Statement
Zynga	"We founded Zynga in 2007 with the mission of connecting the world through games. We believed play—like search, share and shop—would become one of the core activities on the internet." www.sec.gov/Archives/edgar/data/1439404/000119312511343682/ d198836d424b4.htm
Pandora	"Our mission is to enrich people's lives by enabling them to enjoy music they know and discover music they'll love, anytime, anywhere. People connect with music on a fundamentally personal and deeply emotional level. Whether it's a song someone first heard 10 years ago or one they've just discovered, if they connect with that music on our service, a strong bond is forged at that moment with Pandora. Just as we value music, we also hold a deep respect for those who create it. We celebrate and hold dear the individuals who have chosen to make music, from megastars to talented new and emerging artists." www.sec.gov/Archives/edgar/data/1230276/000119312511165534/ d424b4.htm

---

[4] Western Union internal memo (1876)

Company	Mission Statement
Zillow	"Our mission is to build the most trusted and vibrant home-related marketplace to empower consumers with information and tools to make intelligent decisions about homes." www.sec.gov/Archives/edgar/data/1334814/000119312511192519/d424b4.htm
Amazon.com	"Our vision is to be earth's most customer centric company; to build a place where people can come to find and discover anything they might want to buy online." http://phx.corporate-ir.net/phoenix.zhtml?c=97664&p=irol-faq#14296
Starbucks	"Our mission: to inspire and nurture the human spirit—one person, one cup and one neighborhood at a time." www.starbucks.com/about-us/company-information/mission-statement/
Nike	"To bring inspiration and innovation to every athlete in the world." http://help-us.nike.com/app/answers/detail/a_id/113/~/what-is-nike's-mission-statement%3F
Google	"To organize the world's information and make it universally accessible and useful." www.google.com/about/company/

Have Passion for What You Do

You may have a great mission but it must be something you are extremely passionate about. If not, it will be mostly hollow. As a blogger for Forbes.com, I hear a lot of pitches from startup entrepreneurs and it is usually clear when they are not excited about their mission or that they do not even have one!

I can only select a few startups about which to write, and they need to catch my attention quickly. If the first few sentences of their pitch e-mail are not interesting, I'll probably just transfer the message to the "Media" section of my Gmail account. Rarely do I look back at any of them. And even those companies that pique my interest and with which I agree to set up a meeting to hear what they have to say, I find that many of the presentations are lackluster. The founders usually spend too much time on their background and the technology of their product. When it comes to explaining their company's vision and strategy, their message is usually muddled, which is an ominous sign. Based on my experience, I know that many of these companies eventually just fizzle out.

I could go on for several pages documenting all the dud presentations I've seen and heard, but let's focus on the positive, shall we? Let's look at one of the exchanges I've had that stood out. In September 2007, I had a phone interview with Mint.com's founder, Aaron Patzer. The company, as most people know by now, allows users to manage their finances better by importing their financial information from banks and credit cards into one central database. Mint.com then provides helpful reports, charts, and financial tips and suggestions to its users.

Although the product itself was intriguing—and a possible disruption to Intuit's Quicken franchise—this was not what made the call memorable. Instead, it was Patzer's pure enthusiasm for what he had created. He talked about how Quicken didn't work for him and how he wanted a product that could help solve his own problems with managing his finances. Simply put, Patzer had made it his *mission* to make it easier for people to manage their finances.

During a later demonstration of the product, Patzer showed me his personal Mint.com account. His enthusiastic presentation revealed that he had a classic case of "eating his own dog food"—that is, he had become a passionate user of his own product. What's more, by showing me that he, himself, used Mint.com to manage his personal finances, Patzer was making another statement to bolster his product: It was secure. Security is a big-time concern for users, but Patzer talked about some of the Herculean efforts he had made to ensure that Mint.com would keep its users' personal financial information safe. All in all, it was an impressive demonstration and I was not surprised that Mint.com became an instant hit. Fearing the disruption, Intuit shelled out $170 million to buy Mint.com in September 2009.

Although passion is not a prerequisite for success—I personally think nothing really is—passion is high on my list of factors that ultimately help good companies thrive. Passion is infectious. It fosters enthusiasm among the employees, the customers, and the media. It's a powerful force. Perhaps most important, passion helps founders maintain their drive to work hard and succeed. Wouldn't you rather spend your time working on something you love? No wonder top entrepreneurs often say they would work for free.

There are few entrepreneurs who are more passionate about what they do than Rick Alden, who took up skiing at a young age in 1970 and then got hooked on snowboarding in 1985. Wanting to bolster the sport, Alden formed National Snowboard, a marketing company that specialized in snowboarding events. Ultimately, National Snowboard's work became a key factor in making the sport a huge success. After he sold the company in the mid 1990s, Alden then started Device Manufacturing, which focused on developing snowboard boots and bindings. He sold that company as well. Then, in 2003, Alden got the idea for his next venture, and it would be his breakout hit. At the time, he was listening to his iPod while on a chairlift in Park City, Utah, and he wondered: Why aren't there premium headphones for this device? Again, Alden wasted little time and started a company called Skullcandy. In the company's early days, it was not easy to get traction in the market, but he was persistent. It was his passion, after all! Over time, Skullcandy caught on and became a top lifestyle brand. By 2010, sales reached $35.7 million; a year later, the company went public. Cool, huh?

Let's look at another example. When Zuckerberg started Facebook, it was not his full-time gig. He was a student at Harvard and had his hands full with a number of other projects, one of which was Wirehog, an app that enabled users to share files of all types, with a focus on music files, and Zuckerberg found it to be more interesting than Facebook. Even as Facebook began to take off, Zuckerberg still thought Wirehog would be his breakout idea. Eventually, though, he realized it was a mistake and abandoned the project. Wirehog never caught on, and this was probably for the best, because Zuckerberg was concerned that entertainment companies might sue him and his company for copyright infringement. In addition to Facebook and Wirehog, Zuckerberg created a tool called *Synapse*, which played music based on user's interests and which caught the eye of companies like Microsoft. He also built some other highly popular apps, all of which allowed users to share with one another. CourseMatch, for example, made it easy to see who was taking what courses in a given semester, whereas Facemesh showed pictures of two students of the same gender side by side and allowed viewers to vote on who was the more attractive of the two. Even though not all of his programs and applications proved to be enduring, the fact is that all of Zuckerberg's entrepreneurial activities revolved around his deep passion for coding and his special interest in creating apps that allowed for sharing with other people. The software apps he developed were tools that allowed him to pursue his goal of connecting and sharing with others.

Be Committed to What You Do

Changing the world is not a part-time gig. It needs to be an obsession. When Jeff Bezos saw an opportunity to create an e-commerce company that sells books, he quit his high-paying job as a hedge fund manager, took his family across the country to Seattle, and along the way created the business plan for Amazon.com. Bezos (rightly) thought the Internet was a megatrend. Zuckerberg had a similar experience. He and several of his Harvard pals left school during the summer of 2004 and rented a house in Palo Alto to build Facebook. There was not much of a plan but he wanted to devote his full attention to the website. By the end of the year, he decided to drop out of college.

These stories are fairly common. Consider Steve Streit, who lost his job in 1999 as a disc jockey. At the time, he had six kids and no job lined up. But he was passionate about his idea for a prepaid debit card. He put all his savings into creating a company, called Green Dot, to realize his dream. He eventually raised venture capital, struck a major distribution agreement with Walmart and took the company public in 2010 at a billion dollar valuation.

An entrepreneur needs to be highly committed and focused. Distractions can be fatal. True, there are some exceptions. Steve Jobs was able to run Apple and Pixar at the same time. But as we all know, people like Steve Jobs do not come around often.

Aim High

As an up-and-coming entrepreneur, you need to care more about your mission than you do about anything else—including your company. Marc Bennioff, the founder of Salesforce.com, certainly does. I had a chance to talk to Bennioff during the early days when he founded his company, and I watched as its growth skyrocketed. For the most part, Salesforce.com created software for customer relationship management (CRM). CRM software is not very exciting to most people, but Bennioff found a unique way to deliver it to companies: He pioneered the cloud computing model, which meant that companies could access Bennioff's CRM software via the Internet. This approach to distribution was disruptive, because traditionally software was installed on corporate networks and required lots of hardware and servers—not to mention high-paid consultants. Bennioff was convinced that the cloud would be much better. When I spoke with Bennioff, he rarely mentioned CRM. Instead, he railed against traditional software. To me, this was a much more interesting message than hearing about the features of a CRM suite.

As I got to know others at Salesforce.com, I quickly realized that they also deeply understood the company's message about the power of cloud-computing and believed in it. There was never any confusion regarding this when I was talking to someone from Salesforce.com. Over time, Salesforce.com became the symbol of cloud computing. When businesses decided they wanted to adopt cloud-based solutions, the first place they turned was Salesforce.com. This brand advantage has allowed Salesforce.com to expand its platform to other software categories. As of 2012, Salesforce.com has a market value of more than $20 billion.

Think Big

Many entrepreneurs want lifestyle businesses, which are not focused on strong growth. It is really about having an operation that provides enough profits to allow much more time for other interests. Who wouldn't want to run a web site from, say, Maui, and spend a few hours a day working? Some people actually do this, and the endeavor can be lucrative, but these types of businesses do not generate much wealth. In this book, I look at those businesses that create wealth that is *life changing*. This means that there is often little time for anything but the business, so it helps to be passionate about the business in the first place.

Building a megabusiness may seem like a huge risk, but there are certainly some benefits from doing so. For example, large companies have a much easier time recruiting talent. Who doesn't want to work for a company that has a big opportunity ahead of it? In addition, it is much easier to secure venture capital if you are seeking funding to create a large company. Few venture capitalists (VCs) even consider supporting a company that is gunning for a market opportunity less than $1 billion. For them, investing in smaller companies is just not worth the risk.

Despite this basic reality, I run into a lot of entrepreneurs who do not realize the importance of size and who try constantly to nab introductions to VCs to no avail. I do my best to steer them in the right direction and mention that they might need to rethink their goals—that is, to think on a grand scale. For the most part, thinking big is not easy for entrepreneurs, and as a result, their efforts to raise venture capital are often quixotic.

Now, thinking big does not mean you become a success automatically, but doing so will likely give you some downside protection. How? Let's consider an example: Suppose you start a company that is focused on a market that has a $2 billion potential. After several years of hard work, you reach revenues of $50 million. Although your company is nowhere near to becoming the next Facebook, you have still achieved a great outcome and your company certainly has value! Now let's say you decide to sell it. Even if you do not make a substantial amount from this deal, because your VCs will probably get the lion's share from the sale, you are still considered "bankable." You can take your lessons learned from this experience and then roll them over into your next venture. You probably have a few million bucks in the bank, as well, to start your next business.

This is the process that Mark Pincus, one of the original investors in Facebook, went through with several ho-hum startups. However, by 2007, he had leveraged his experience and network to create Zynga. By late 2011, he had raised $1 billion in an IPO and was put on the Forbes Billionaires List.

Someone else who thinks big is Elon Musk, who has affected various industries and millions of people across the world. His entrepreneurial journey has been far from easy—and his ventures have endured several near-death experiences— but he has learned from every step along the way. Musk started coding when he was 10 years old. He sold his first program, a game about space, 2 years later for $500. Then, in the mid 1990s, Musk started an Internet content publisher, called *Zip2*, which he sold for $300 million. His next venture was X.com, which focused on online financial services. To bolster growth, he merged the company with rival Confinity, which was cofounded by Max Levchin and Peter Thiel (the latter was an original investor in Facebook). The new company became known as *PayPal*, but it had a high burn rate and nearly ran out of cash. Thiel managed to raise some much-needed capital in April 2000. The company went public and was sold for $1.5 billion to eBay in late 2002.

Although Musk could have retired easily after the sale of PayPal, he was still restless to change the world, so he invested much of his net worth in several megaconcepts. One was Tesla Motors, which develops electric cars. However, during the financial crisis of 2008, the company very nearly went bankrupt, endangering Musk's finances in the process. Somehow, though, Musk was able to raise enough capital to save the company, and in June 2010, he took Tesla Motors public in the first IPO of a U.S. automaker since Ford went public in the mid 1950s.

Meanwhile, at the same time that Musk was building Tesla, he was also creating SpaceX, which develops space launch vehicles. He used innovative engineering techniques to accelerate the manufacturing process and snagged a $1.6 billion contract from the National Aeronautics and Space Administration. In May 2012, SpaceX launched and delivered cargo successfully to the international space station. The only others to do so include the governments of the United States, Russia, and China. Oh, and Musk is only 40 years old.

Be Prepared to Fail

It's a gruesome fact that most startups fail. They go absolutely nowhere. In light of this reality, it is amazing that entrepreneurs even start companies. Something must be wrong with them, right? Well, maybe entrepreneurs are wired differently. Although most people are risk averse, entrepreneurs *love* risk. They thrive on it. More important, to the most successful entrepreneurs, failure is not a stopping point. Instead, it represents yet another learning experience along the path to eventual success.

Even Zuckerberg has had his share of failures. Did you know that Facebook tried to launch a social network for the workplace? It was a disaster. So was Zuckerberg's early mobile product, which used SMS (short message service) messaging to access Facebook. It was so complicated that people needed a chart to understand the functions. Then there was Beacon, which was a downright terrible idea. Beacon showed a user's purchases to his or her friends, which created lots of problems; some people even found out about their birthday and Christmas presents! Beacon was so bad that it tarnished Facebook's reputation, but Zuckerberg learned from these experiences and became stronger.

Success is a paradox: If you are not failing, then you are not succeeding. No one is perfect, including history's standout business leaders like Steve Jobs and Bill Gates. Table 1-2 presents a few examples of people who made mistakes but still came out on top.

Table 1-2. Examples of Businessmen Who Failed

Individuals	Failures
Kevin Systrom and Michel Krieger	Systrom and Krieger's first product, Burbn, was a failure, but they learned some valuable lessons and went on to create Instagram.
Bill Gates and Paul Allen	The first startup of Gates and Allen was Traf-O-Data, which found little traction.
Steve Jobs	Jobs got kicked out of Apple in the mid 1980s. He then started Pixar and NeXT, both of which struggled during their early years and Jobs nearly went bankrupt.
Walt Disney	Disney was fired from a job at a newspaper because his editor said he lacked imagination and had no good ideas. Disney started several businesses that went bankrupt.

When you experience a failure, keep that experience at the forefront of your mind. Try to learn helpful lessons from it. Failure isn't fun, but the process can be extremely valuable, which reminds me of a true story. I won't go into the names of the founders or the companies they created. Those details are not important. Rather, the lessons that were learned in the aftermath of the failure are what's key.

Let's rewind to the start of the Internet boom, in 1994. Two entrepreneurs, Jane and Joe, started their own Internet companies, both of which grew quickly. The market was certainly big enough for several strong players, and the founders were able to raise several rounds of venture capital before taking their respective companies public. By the late 1990s, Jane and Joe were both worth billions. Then, suddenly, the Internet market gave way—and so did the valuations; Jane and Joe were now facing possible bankruptcy. To avoid the collapse of their companies, they raised money at low valuations and had to fire hundreds of people, many of whom were friends. It was an agonizing experience. However, what happened next was crucial. Joe saw the experience as a failure and became risk adverse. Even though his company was beginning to experience growth again, he moved his business along at a slow pace. He tried to avoid any long-term commitments, such as investing in new technologies or hiring people. Joe ultimately sold his company for about $700 million. True, this is a great deal, but it could have been much better.

You see, Jane did just the opposite. She continued to believe that her opportunity was huge, and she started to get aggressive with her investments. She hired more employees. She even struck several large acquisitions to add new products and customers. It was risky, but Jane's company's growth *exploded*. When Joe was selling his company for $700 million, Jane was selling hers for nearly $7 billion.

Put It All Together

The content of blogs like Techcrunch, VentureBeat, and Pandodaily, and the stories about the entrepreneurs in this book may be intimidating to aspiring entrepreneurs. How can you compete? How can you raise the financing? Is your idea good enough? How do you build the right team? Before you get too overwhelmed, it is important to take some deep breaths and think about how other great entrepreneurs got their start. Steve Jobs and Steve Wozniak started Apple in a garage. Mark Zuckerberg started Facebook in a dorm. So, what is it that sets the Jobs, Wozniaks, and Zuckerbergs of the world apart? The answer is this: These founders started small, but they had lots of energy, passion, and focus. They also had little or no business or startup experience. Instead, they figured things out along the way.

So think big, but start small. As seen in the chapter, the "big" part is the mission, which should always be the driving force of the company. You should also be exceptionally passionate about it— almost becoming an obsession. Is your mission something you would quit your job for? If not, you probably should keep your job.

In the next chapter, we'll get deeper into the process of building your venture. We'll take a look at making sure you build a solid legal foundation.

Legal Structure

A verbal contract isn't worth the paper it's written on.

—Samuel Goldwyn

Like many smart young software engineers, Mark Zuckerberg did a lot of contract work for an array of clients while he was in college. Often, these gigs were short term in nature, but they tended to generate thousands of dollars for him. In fact, the money actually helped him pay his way through Harvard.

However, Zuckerberg did not understand the risks of these engagements. What if he developed a product or program that ultimately conflicted with the creation of Facebook? Might he be giving away his valuable intellectual property? As it turned out, the contract work that Zuckerberg undertook as a college student turned out to be a real source of legal problems for him and his young company, and Zuckerberg ended up making some big-time legal mistakes that cost Facebook dearly before he got the help of a qualified attorney.

In this chapter, we take a look at the legal blunders Zuckerberg made during his company's infancy, as well as several strategies he could have used to avoid the many infamous legal headaches that Facebook has suffered. As you're reading, soak up the legal lessons of this chapter and learn from Zuckerberg and Facebook's mistakes, because nothing can bring a young company to its knees faster than a lawsuit (or 12). Just look at Napster.

Obtain Legal Services

When starting a new venture, it's tempting to scrimp on legal fees. Why should anyone get hundreds of dollars per hour for their services? Aren't the majority of legal issues that startups face fairly straightforward?

Not really. The law is critically important in any business endeavor, and the legal details of even the most everyday business transactions can get extremely complicated. Despite this well-known reality, many entrepreneurs still try to go solo when it comes to their legal issues, and they rely on a free Google search rather than a paid legal professional. They also try to find sample contracts online and then attempt to tailor them to their business's needs. Obviously, this inadvisable practice can cause a world of trouble for young startups, because these legal documents may have already been negotiated or may be aligned with the laws of a jurisdiction other than that in which they operate.

Some founders, acquiescing to the necessity of obtaining some form of legal advice for their company, use third-party legal services like LegalZoom. Although companies like LegalZoom provide tremendous services at cost-efficient prices, they are often incapable of meeting adequately the needs of a technical startup with specialized issues that include the need to protect intellectual property. In addition, the fact that online legal services are named as such is a bit misleading, because they do not provide actual legal services. More accurately, they are document preparation services—and very good ones, at that—but you should not rely on them to serve as your company's legal counsel.

No doubt, your best solution is to hire a qualified attorney who specializes in technical startups to advise your company in the many legal challenges it will undoubtedly face. Startup attorneys not only understand the nuances and landmines that are part and parcel of building a new venture, but they also realize that startups have little capital to spare. As a result, technical startup attorneys are usually willing to take equity as payment for their legal fees during a startup's early days. Facebook, for example, issued 1.29% in equity to its first law firm.

Aside from sparing you the need to fork over huge amounts of cash in your company's infancy, paying your attorney in equity effectively aligns their interests with those of your company. In other words, your attorney wants to see her equity in your company expand, effectively leading her to provide you with better legal counsel, which is a win–win for all involved. Also, most likely, you won't be your technical startup attorney's first client, which means that she probably has lots of contacts in the technology startup industry and might even be willing to make key introductions to potential investors.

Prior to hiring an attorney, make sure you perform some due diligence on your candidate pool. First, get a list of each candidate's clients—either from fellow entrepreneurs or services like Avvo—and call them. Doing so is a good way to get a better sense of the caliber of the attorneys. Here are some other suggestions:

- Make sure you negotiate the attorney's fees, and never take the first offer that she makes. This type of negotiation is actually expected and even customary.

- Insist that a partner work on your account, not a junior associate. Although you'll pay a higher rate for the counsel of a partner, the quality of the work will be much better.

- Put a cap on admissible attorney's fees. Why give a lawyer an excuse to keep billing and billing?

- Remember that attorneys are naturally conservative and have a tendency to focus on all the ways in which you and your company could get into legal trouble. So, when your attorney gives you legal advice, make sure you ask questions such as "What are the chances of getting in trouble?" and "What would be the consequences?" If the potential fallout seems minor or worth the risk, then you should purse that course of action even if an attorney has some doubts about it. Business is about taking calculated risks.

Now let's take a look at Zuckerberg's experience with obtaining legal counsel. Although Zuckerberg's contract programming work was certainly helpful to him and Facebook, because it enabled him to build his business savvy and learn his craft, one of his contract projects turned into a legal nightmare for the company. In November 2003, twin brothers Cameron and Tyler Winklevoss as well as Divya Narendra met with Zuckerberg to develop a web site called *HarvardConnection*, which would host a list of upcoming parties and provide discounts for nightclubs. The Winklevosses and Narendra agreed to let Zuckerberg in on the deal. There was no written contract between the four parties, but there were many e-mail and instant messages that indicated that they had arrived at some type of agreement—part of which was, in exchange for equity in the enterprise, Zuckerberg would create the web site for HarvardConnection.

Zuckerberg was immediately given access to HarvardConnection's server. However, despite stating initially that the job would be an easy one to complete, he failed to make much appreciable headway on the project. He claimed that he was swamped with schoolwork, but assured the Winklevosses and Narendra that he was working steadily on the site. Meanwhile, without ever having created functional code for HarvardConnection, Zuckerberg registered the domain name thefacebook.com and launched his own social networking site, which later became the phenomenon we all know today as Facebook. Upon hearing of Zuckerberg's web site, the Winklevosses and Narendra quickly filed a lawsuit, claiming that Zuckerberg stole their idea for a social network (they eventually created a college site called ConnectU). The litigation was finally settled in early 2008 for an estimated $65 million.

This experience was a classic, expensive mess, and Zuckerberg could have avoided this legal headache by taking a few simple precautions. First of all, after agreeing to work with the Winklevosses and Narendra on their web site, he could have insisted on a written contract and asked an attorney to review it prior to signing it. When becoming a partner in a new venture, it is essential that you sign a document that outlines each partner's rights and responsibilities. Prior contract work and former jobs are often sources of problems for entrepreneurs who start new ventures, so think hard about your legal exposure—and about what papers you should or should not sign. Here's some advice:

- Nondisclosure Agreement (NDA): Under the terms of an NDA, you cannot disclose material information to third parties—in general, for a fixed period of time, say, a year or two. These contracts can be broad but are usually enforceable. If you have signed an NDA and then start a company that is similar to your employer's or your client's, then the NDA could be a problem. Even if there is not an NDA in effect, the employer or client may be able to claim misappropriation of trade secrets. As a general rule, then, be wary about using propriety information when creating your own venture. Doing so could result in a nasty lawsuit.

- Noncompete: Under the terms of a noncompete agreement, you cannot compete against your employer or client for a set period of time—often a couple years. The good news is that noncompete agreements are generally not enforceable in California, but this is not the case with many other states. It's yet another reason to create a company in California. Keep in mind, though, that if you signed a noncompete agreement as part of an acquisition, you may be held accountable if you do not abide by its terms. After all, you likely received payment for your efforts.

- Work-for-Hire: Typically found as a clause in a contractor's agreement, a work-for-hire forces you to relinquish your right to the intellectual property to any work or product that you create for a client. Work-for-hires could cause you huge problems if you go on to form your own business based on work you completed for somebody else. Thus, if you plan to do contract work, it is probably best to avoid doing so in an area on which you plan to focus when you start your own venture. If you're an employee at a company, you will probably be asked to sign an invention assignment. Like work-for-hires, invention assignments give full ownership to your employer to all the intellectual property you create on the job. Some companies may even extend the time period in which this type of agreement is in effect beyond your last day of employment, such as for 6 months to 1 year. California, however, has some wiggle room. For example, if you create an invention during off hours, do not use company resources to invent it, and it is not relevant to your company's business, then the employer has no ownership rights to it. An invention agreement may require that you disclose your activities, though.

- Nonsolicitation: This type of agreement states that you are not allowed to poach the customers or suppliers of your employer. Interestingly enough, California looks unfavorably on these types of arrangements. Leaving an employer to form a startup is typical in Silicon Valley. In other words, even if you sign and ignore a nonsolicitation agreement in California, your former employer may not subject you to any litigation. In some cases, entrepreneurs may even get an investment from their original employer or may put together a customer or partnership arrangement. However, you should still be cautious when signing this type of agreement.

- Stock Options: If you work for a high-tech company, then make sure you understand your rights regarding your stock options when you leave the company. A stock options agreement usually permits you 90 days to exercise your vested options, but the sooner you do this, the better.

Consider Incorporation

When should you incorporate? There are no magical answers to this question, and it seems—at least when it comes to legal matters—that this is typically the case. Here are some common triggers to consider incorporation:

- Hiring employees or contractors
- Talking to potential customers
- Talking to potential investors
- Securing a cofounder or two

These four triggers are all serious steps in creating a company, and it is much easier to pursue these efforts under the guise of a corporation. If nothing else, being incorporated lends you more credibility when talking to potential employees and investors, because they'll know you have a certain level of commitment to the venture.

Here are some benefits of being incorporated:

- A corporation is critical when hiring noncitizens or nonresidents, because obtaining a visa is easier for these individuals if the business for which they are working is incorporated. In addition, international talent has become vitally important for technical startups.

- A corporation makes it easier to issue stock options, which is critical for technical startups.

- A corporation provides liability protection and ensures that the investors and officers are not held personally responsible for any debts or claims made against the corporation. Keep in mind, though, that you are not protected if you fail to maintain the formalities of the corporation, such as conducting board meetings and publishing an annual report.

If you incorporate your company earlier in its life span, you may also be required to pay less taxes if and when it comes time to sell. How is this so? Consider that if you own stock for more than 1 year before selling it, any gains you accrue on the sale are subject to a maximum federal taxation rate of 15% (not including any taxes levied by your state). If you do not hold the stock for at least a year, then you pay taxes at the ordinary rates, the maximum of which is 35%. For example, suppose you incorporate your business on January 1, 2012, and then launch your product in November 2012. Then, in February 2013, you decide to sell your company for $2 million. In this situation, you would get taxed at 15% because your shares in the company are more than 12 months old. It's true that it may cost several thousand dollars to incorporate, and there are always ongoing expenses and filings involved with incorporating. However, when it comes to your venture, incorporation is a smart move—a move that, in the end, could save you potentially millions of dollars.

Each state has its own corporate laws and has a variety of structures, such as a C-Corp, a Limited Liability Company (LLC), and an S-Corp. The differences among them may seem arcane, but often have to do with taxes and the need to conform to certain business formalities, like conducting board meetings, as mentioned earlier. For example, LLCs have minimal filing and administrative requirements, which result in lower taxes for the company. Perhaps this is why Facebook's co-founder Eduardo Saverin originally formed Facebook as an LLC.

Unfortunately for Saverin, whose main role at the company was to help with business matters, this was a wrong decision. If he had thought far enough into the future, he might have been able to guess that Facebook would eventually need to raise outside capital, which means establishing Facebook as a C-Corp, preferably one in Delaware. Delaware C-Corps don't just make it easier to obtain financing; they also are streamlined for setting up option plans, which allow a company to provide equity compensation to employees. Furthermore, the state of Delaware is home to many corporations specifically because it has a well-developed set of corporate laws, and the judges in that state also tend to act quickly on legal matters.

While some attorneys may quibble, I think a Delaware C-Corp is the best option for technology startups.

When forming one, the following are some things to consider:

- Establish each partner's roles and responsibilities within the corporation. Here, again, is an opportunity to learn from Facebook's mistakes. Saverin maintained control of the LLC, and when he had a dispute with Zuckerberg, he actually froze the corporation's bank account. This heedless action almost killed Facebook, and Zuckerberg and his father had to put up $85,000 of their own capital to keep it afloat.

- Maintain control of your stock. Just look what happened to Craigslist. In 2004, one of Craigslist's employees sold a 28.5% stake in the company to eBay, which turned out to be a terrible situation for Craigslist, because eBay eventually came out with its own classified service. Craigslist would never have been in this mess, however, if it had set stock resale restrictions. If Craigslist had given itself the right of first refusal—or, in other words, the option to buy shares of its own stock at the same price and terms that a third party is willing to pay—it could have avoided this horrible situation altogether.

- Assign all the intellectual property to the corporation. If you don't, the entity has little value and investors may not be willing to make any commitments to it. Furthermore, if you have a cofounder and fail to assign all the corporation's intellectual property to the entity itself, the cofounder could very well take her intellectual property and go elsewhere with it. Consider that when Facebook was created, Zuckerberg did not assign the intellectual property to the LLC. As a result, the entity had little value, except for some money in a bank account.

Determine How to Split Equity Before the Need Arises

When forming a company, the founders are often optimistic and friendly—and with due cause. Hey, it's an exciting time—full of huge amounts of potential. However, all this shared excitement can cloud your judgment. As much as possible, you need to realize that, over time, there are bound to be disputes between you and your cofounder. This very scenario cropped up fairly quickly in the case of Facebook, given Zuckerberg's early clashes with Saverin. In some cases, these disputes can result in either you or your cofounder leaving the company. In light of this, you need to think about protecting your interests, which means negotiating hard with your cofounders. A key issue is making sure you allocate the equity in a way that motivates your team but is not too generous that it risks harming the venture.

The nonconfrontational approach to this issue is to split everything equally, but this may be the wrong way. For example, suppose one founder has quit his job to dedicate himself fully to the venture whereas the other founder is still working a nine-to-five job and can only commit time to the company after hours and on weekends. In this case, it would not be fair for the founders to split the equity evenly. Or suppose one founder is bringing existing code or customers or cash to the table. Would it make sense in this situation for each founder to be compensated equally? Probably not.

Equity-sharing discussions can be uncomfortable—and even contentious—but they may provide some insight into the real personalities of your cofounders. You may even realize that they may not be a good fit! As for Facebook, there was a difference in the equity split, with Zuckerberg getting a 65% share, Saverin getting a 30% share, and Dustin Moskovitz (who became involved in Facebook later in its development but is still considered one of its original cofounders) receiving a 5% share in the company.

Use Vested Founders' Stock

Suppose you start a business with three other cofounders. Everyone works extremely hard, except one person: George. He rarely does any coding and when he does get involved, he usually complains. He's actually become a liability to the venture. You and your other cofounders want to push him out of the company. The problem is that he owns 25% of the company's stock. In other words, he is, essentially, getting a free ride based on the efforts of everyone else. It's unfair, right? Absolutely. However, fairness in this case does not matter to a judge. George paid for his stock and in return received 25% ownership. It's that simple.

However, there is one way to deal with this type of situation—by using vested founders' stock. Here's how it works: Suppose your company has 1 million shares, and you and your other three cofounders have decided that each founder receives 250,000 of those shares. The price per share is 1¢, so each founder pays $2,500 to capitalize the venture. Then, in your company's shareholder agreement, you include a vesting schedule that stipulates that a founder has to wait at least 1 year to vest—or obtain ownership—of the first 62,500 shares of his investment. The rest of his shares will vest, each month, for 3 more years.

Now let's return to your hypothetical venture and, of course, George. You and your cofounders have been busting your butts and it has become readily apparent during that first year that you've been working together that George is just not working as hard as the rest of you. Because you and your cofounders were forward-thinking when you formed your company and decided to reimburse each cofounder for his work with vested founders' stock, you can buy George out of his percentage of stock much more easily than if you had given him an outright share in the company.

Vested founders' stock is a common business approach for Silicon Valley startups, and it works quite well for most parties involved—the Georges of the world notwithstanding. In fact, when a VC firm makes an investment in a company, the firm usually requires that the company begin using vested founders' stock. If a venture already has a vesting program in place, it is unlikely that a VC firm will seek to undo this policy. The use of vested founders' stock also shows the VC that the company's founders are forward-thinking.

In some cases, especially among technical startups, one or more of the company's cofounders has already worked hard on the product before the other cofounders decide to jump onboard. Because of this unique situation, the company's original cofounders may get credit for their early work by vesting a certain percentage of their stock, say, 5%, at the time of the company's incorporation.

Termination and Change of Control

Sometimes companies with vested founders' stock use a vesting schedule that accelerates when one of its founders is terminated without cause. In this type of situation, the terminated founder typically walks away from the venture with all of his shares in the company. In theory, this arrangement seems to make sense. After all, if a founder didn't do anything explicitly wrong in his work for the venture, it isn't exactly fair for him to be fired and receive no compensation for the time and energy he invested in the company.

In reality, however, the case law for how to define *cause* is far from clear-cut, which means that even if you had due cause for terminating a founder, that founder would be able to claim that you didn't have due cause and would walk away with a big chunk of your company. This doesn't seem quite fair, either, now, does it? As a result, my suggestion is to avoid accelerated vesting schedules at all costs. However, if accelerated vesting is important to you and your cofounders, there is a better approach—partial acceleration. When your company uses partially accelerated vesting schedules, you maintain much more control over how many shares leave your company when one of your cofounders is forced out. For example, your company policy could be that founders who are terminated without cause are given an accelerated vesting schedule, but only for 6 months of that schedule.

Accelerated vesting is also used in change-of-control events, such as when your company is acquired by another firm. If you and your cofounders believe that a change of control over your company may be likely, you can incorporate into your shareholder agreement a single-trigger acceleration clause, which states that the forthcoming event will trigger the acceleration of 100% of your stock options. Keep in mind, however, that a single-trigger acceleration clause may make it nearly impossible to sell your company, because potential buyers will likely be put off by a stipulation that allows the founders to walk away from the sale with a huge payoff.

If you would like to provide for yourself in the event of a change of control but are wary of using a single-trigger acceleration clause for the reasons mentioned here, you might instead choose to include one or more of the following options in your shareholder agreement:

- Double-trigger clause: There must be a change of control and a termination without cause (often for a term of 12 months) for there to be 100% vesting.

- Compromise: At the time of the change of control, a partial amount of the shares will vest automatically, and then the rest are subject to a double trigger.

- Severance: The shares vest completely after the cofounders have been with the new company for a period of time, such as 1 to 2 years.

83(b) election

As most Americans would agree, taxes involve mind-numbing paperwork and onerous payments—and this is especially true for startups that don't understand the Internal Revenue Service's (IRS's) core principles and choose to distribute vested founders' stock. To avoid experiencing a big-time tax bite, read on.

Continuing with our example presented earlier in this section, "Use Vested Founders' Stock," let's suppose that your company has been in business for 1 year, which means that 62,500 of your 250,000 shares have vested. However, instead of its initial price of 1¢ per share, your company's stock value has increased to $1 per share because the venture has made a lot of progress. Thanks to you and your cofounders' hard work, the IRS will now tax you on your gain. In your case, your gain is $62,500 ($1 for every share that is vested) less the initial $2,500 investment you paid (known as the *cost basis*), or $60,000. To make matters worse, the IRS continues to tax your vested founders' stock as it vests over time.

Yes, you owe tax on this gain in share price, even though it is probably nearly impossible for you to sell your shares. The IRS does not really care if you don't have the cash to pay your gains tax, either. It just sets up some type of payment program for you in the hopes that you eventually pay off the full taxed amount to the government.

This is an ugly situation for sure, but if you file an 83(b) election with the IRS, you can avoid the whole mess. How is this so? When you file an 83(b) election, you are—for tax purposes—treating your stock as though it was fully vested at the time your startup was formed. As a result, you pay taxes on the amount your stock was worth when you initially purchased it, rather than waiting to pay taxes on it until it appreciates down the line. Therefore, if you had filed an 83(b) election at the outset of your company's formation after paying 1¢ per share to get your venture going, your gains tax would have been $0 when the price per share rose to $1 a year later.

By using the 83b election, you also start the clock ticking for long-term capital gains treatment. If you hold on to your stock for more than a year, your maximum tax rate on those shares is 15%. In other words, make sure you file an 83(b). Period. But remember, you must file an 83(b) election within 30 days after purchasing your company's stock. There are no exceptions to this rule, and filing is as simple as sending a letter to the IRS. Don't forget to use certified return receipt to make sure the IRS has received your paperwork. Your company should also keep a copy of the 83(b) so that you can include it with the following year's tax return.

Payment for Stock

When a company is first started, its value is usually minimal, which makes it fairly easy for the founders to buy the company's stock. If you recall from our previous example, each founder had to pay only $2,500 for 250,000 shares of stock, at a price of 1¢ per share. This is a fairly common situation.

Yet even a few thousand dollars can be tough for young founders to spare. Because of this, some founders offer to contribute their intellectual property, such as existing computer code or even a business plan, as payment for the shares. Although substituting intellectual property for cash might seem reasonable, it can cause huge headaches down the road. Not only is intellectual property difficult to value, but the contribution could result in adverse tax consequences for your company. There could even be difficulties in ensuring that the corporation actually owns the intellectual property. Therefore, to keep things clean, the best approach is for all parties to contribute cash. If a founder is serious about the venture, he will find a way to scrounge up a few thousand bucks.

File Your Patents

In March 2012, Yahoo! filed a patent infringement suit against Facebook in an attempt to blunt the social network's progress and delay its IPO. Interestingly, this was not the first time that Yahoo! had engaged in such legal practices. During Google's IPO in 2004, Yahoo! launched a lawsuit against the search engine behemoth and was able to snag shares in the offering as a settlement. And Yahoo! is not the only major player in the tech world that is aggressive in going after the competition in the courtroom. At the time of this writing, operators big and small around the globe are embroiled in patent wars.

Strangely enough, at the time that it was sued by Yahoo!, Facebook was rather lackadaisical about pursuing patent rights. In fact, it had filed for only 60 patents in its 8 years in operation. Facebook, however, did not allow Yahoo! to use a lawsuit to gain an edge in the market. Instead, the company leveraged its resources to fight back. Facebook shelled out $550 million to purchase patents from Microsoft (the company had bought them from AOL for $1.1 billion a few weeks earlier), and it also purchased roughly 750 patents from IBM (the price tag was not disclosed).

How critically important are patents to the tech industry? They are so important that large tech operators have bought rivals for the main purpose of obtaining ownership of their patents. This appears to be the case with Google's $12.5 billion deal for Motorola Mobility Holdings. Or look at Apple. In 2011, the company joined with others in a consortium to pay $4.5 billion for patents from Nortel Networks (which had gone bust).

True, a startup cannot engage in these kinds of massive monetary transactions, but there are certainly ways to protect your company's intellectual property. Think early on about how to obtain patents for your innovations. Owning the intellectual property rights to your inventions may help to blunt patent infringement lawsuits in the future, and it also could increase the core value of your company when you go out to raise funding, sell your company, or go public.

The law has undergone major changes recently with the America Invents Act. If your product is global—and most Web-based products are—then you must file your patent application before you disclose publicly the details of your new technology. Because of this stipulation, it often makes sense to file a provisional patent, which gives you a grace period of 1 year before requiring that you file a full-blown patent. A provisional patent is not particularly difficult to file, and it also is affordable (the filings fees are $250 or less). Regardless of the type of patent you decide to file, however, it is important that you obtain the assistance of an attorney that specializes in intellectual property law before attempting to file a patent yourself. The complexities of intellectual property law can be mind numbing.

Think Creatively About Your Company Name, Register Your Trademark, and Secure Your URL

One of my favorite t-shirts is from a company called Yammer, which is a social network for businesses (the first investor was Peter Thiel). It seems that whenever I wear it—which just has the logo and the name of the company—some random stranger stops to ask me, "What is Yammer?" One time a woman who must have been in her 70s walked by me and kept saying, "Yammer, Yammer, Yammer." It's catchy, isn't it?

Yammer is, without a doubt, a great company name. Despite how much noise there is in the marketplace, the name Yammer stands out from the crowd. It's memorable, it catches people's attention instantly, and it makes people want to learn more. However, coming up with a striking company name is far from easy. I come across many names that are pretty flat and forgettable. Take Facebook, for instance. Although *Facebook* is a great name, the company's original name was *TheFacebook.com*, which was awkward. Despite some initial resistance, Zuckerberg eventually agreed that "The" was not good for branding.

Company names are crucial, so make sure you spend a lot of time thinking of the right name for your venture. What's more, make sure you can secure the

URL of your company's name, as well as the URL of any of the typical misspellings that might crop up. True, many URLs are already taken, which means you'll probably have to pay off a squatter, (a person who has no plans to use the URL for a website but is only interested in finding a buyer for it) but the purchase of it should be worth it in the end. Facebook had to pay $200,000 for facebook.com and, well, I'd venture to say that the expense was well worth it.

You also need to make sure you can protect your company's name. If not, you may be forced to change it if you lose a trademark dispute, which can be a disaster. It's true that if you start using your company name with an Internet service you start to accrue some rights to the name in what is known as a *common law trademark*; however, these types of trademarks are extremely limited and you are better off filing for a trademark registration with the United States Patent and Trademark Office (USPTO). When you are granted a trademark by the USPTO, you receive presumptive ownership of and protection for the name on a nationwide basis. You also obtain the right to bring an action in federal court to protect the trademark.

There are two types of trademark applications you can file: an in-use application or an intent-to-use application. Many technical startups choose the latter of the two because their Web service typically has not hit the market by the time they file their trademark application. Keep in mind that you can also obtain a trademark for a symbol. Facebook, for example, has a trademark on its logo and the Like button.

Here are some other tips for dealing with trademarks:

- Before applying for a trademark, do a trademark search to determine whether another trademark conflicts with your intended trademark. This process should be conducted by someone who specializes in intellectual property law.

- A trademark cannot be descriptive. Thus, if you create a medical social network, you cannot get a trademark for "Medical Social Network."

- Enforce your trademark. If another company is infringing on it, insist that it cease its infringement. In many cases, companies accomplish this by sending the offender a cease-and-desist letter—a strategy that Facebook has used several times throughout the years. If you fail or choose not to protect your trademark against infringement, you could lose your legal protection for your trademark.

Adhere to Government Regulations

As a social networking company, Facebook deals with many complex laws and regulations, enforceable at both the federal and state levels, involving privacy, data protection, content, protection of minors, and consumer protection. Because Facebook is a global company, it must also deal with the laws of the other countries in which it operates—laws that are often vague and subject to change. All these layers of legal complications can make it tough for Facebook to understand its liability exposures and to operate within the constraints of the law. To this end, Facebook assembled a top-notch legal team. In October 2008, the company hired Theodore Ullyot as its general counsel. Prior to joining Facebook, Ullyot was a partner at Kirkland & Ellis. He was also the chief of staff at the U.S. Justice Department and deputy assistant to then-President George W. Bush. He was even a law clerk for Supreme Court Justice Antonin Scalia. Facebook also brought on a key board member to help with its complicated legal issues: Erskine Bowles. Besides enjoying a successful career in the financial services industry prior to joining Facebook, Bowles also served as White House Chief of Staff from 1996 to 1998.

Of course, it's impractical for a fledgling startup to hire such high-caliber personnel early in its development. However, it is important to be mindful of some of the key regulatory problems that can occur when running a Web or mobile service, especially when dealing with data on consumers. If you do not follow the letter of the law, you may be subjected to severe legal liabilities. But the law is specialized and is evolving. This is why it is important to hire an experienced attorney.

For example, in late 2011, Facebook struck a 20-year settlement with the Federal Trade Commission regarding the company's publishing of its users' information, which violated their privacy rights. The terms of the agreement involved meeting certain ongoing requirements and biannual, independent privacy audits—which, let me tell you, is no walk in the park. It's not clear why Facebook violated the regulations but it shows that there are consequences to misusing user data. You should also be aware that, depending on the platform on which you build your technical service, you may also be subject to *that* platform's privacy rules. One mobile app company—Path—learned this the hard way. David Morin, a former Apple employee and early employee at Facebook, created Path to allow users to build a private social network of no more than 150 friends. As it turned out, however, the app actually sucked up each user's personal information, such as e-mail addresses, names, and phone numbers. The platform that Morin used, Apple iOS, prohibits developers from creating apps that violate its users' privacy rules. Needless to say, an app that allows its developer to access users' contact lists is clearly in violation of Apple's privacy rules.

Apple's CEO Tim Cook was livid and demanded that Morin come to his office, where he got balled out. Interestingly, Path was not the only offender. Other notable companies were doing the same thing, like Yelp, but Path became the "poster boy" of the offense and was used by Apple to set an example. Although these companies continue to operate their services and are highly successful, they are certainly more mindful of Apple's privacy rules. A platform operator like Apple can ban any third-party app it chooses, which could render a company's business model obsolete in an instant.

Consider Other Protections

Bear in mind that patents and trademarks only serve as protection for specific areas of intellectual property. Computer code is usually protected as a trade secret, and to qualify your code as a trade secret, your company must take certain measures. For example, your company should have confidentiality agreements for employees, contractors, and partners. It should also make invention assignment agreements a standard part of its practice. And have a process in place to secure documents.

Consider that when you go for venture funding, your potential investors will do due diligence on matters of ownership. If the ownership of your company's intellectual property is not clear, you may not be able to get the funding you need.

Let Facebook's legal missteps and mistakes be a warning to you. The young startup was embroiled in lawsuit after lawsuit simply because Zuckerberg neglected to think about and guard proactively against potential legal claims that were ultimately brought against the company. Had Zuckerberg refrained from hiring a savvy attorney to mitigate his company's legal problems, the Facebook we know and love today might not have ever gotten off the ground. So do yourself and your company a favor and seek the counsel of a qualified attorney early who understands the nuances of technology startups. When— not *if*, but *when*—a frustrated former employee or a competitor brings the first legal suit against you and your company, you'll understand just how valuable this advice really is.

The Product

Some men see things as they are and say, "Why?" I dream of things that never were and say, "Why not?"

—Robert Kennedy

Mark Zuckerberg is a product genius. He has an innate ability to understand what type of product users will love. Critical to Zuckerberg's success in product development has been his understanding that his product—Facebook—must be aligned with his company's mission of openness and sharing. Zuckerberg describes his company's approach to product development best when he says: "We have found that products that are 'social by design' tend to be more engaging than their traditional counterparts, and we look forward to seeing more of the world's products move in this direction."[1] However, Zuckerberg's imperative to create a social product that promotes openness and sharing may not necessarily fit the mission and ideals of your company. So how do you create a product that squares with your company's mission and yet resonates with your end users? In this chapter, we take a look at the many inputs you can rely on to help you do just that.

Creativity

No matter how hard you try, you can't sit people down in a room and teach them how to be creative. Creativity is a skill that can't be learned, despite the message that countless self-help books and creativity gurus try to sell you. It is similarly erroneous to think, just because you're smart, that you can figure out how to be creative. Creativity has nothing to do with intelligence. In fact,

---

[1] Facebook IPO Prospectus, May 17, 2012, www.sec.gov/Archives/edgar/data/1326801/000119312512240111/d287954d424b4.htm.

some of the most creative people throughout history have had IQs in the normal range.

So, if creativity is not the result of learned knowledge or above-average intelligence, what is it that sets those who are gifted creatively apart from the rest of the pack? Creative people throughout history—like Einstein, Darwin, Mozart, Leonardo da Vinci, and Freud—have been able to bring a fresh perspective to the status quo. They have the innate ability to avoid getting stuck in old, normalized ways of thinking and can, instead, analyze a situation or problem in a new and, ultimately, valuable manner. And as a result of their creative approach to problem solving, they have arrived at some amazing discoveries, as we saw in Chapter 1, when we looked at Samuel Morse's invention of the telegraph.

Add Zuckerberg to the list of figures throughout history who have displayed incredible creative abilities. Part of the reason Zuckerberg has been able to forge creative breakthroughs is because he is a multidimensional person. When he was growing up, he didn't just read programming books. He loved reading the classics, and one of his favorite works of all time is the *Odyssey*. In fact, he could read the classics in their original language—French, Hebrew, Latin, or even ancient Greek. Furthermore, when Zuckerberg went off to college, he didn't just study computer science; he paired this more technical-minded major with another major in psychology.

Yes, Zuckerberg is a fan of liberal arts, and his understanding of and proficiency in this subject matter has most certainly contributed to the creativity he displays when he develops products, solves problems, and runs his market-dominating company. The lesson here is: You never know where inspiration springs from. When Steve Jobs was in college, he took a class on calligraphy. Ever wonder why Apple products come equipped with such beautiful fonts? Now you know the source of the inspiration.

Timing and Some Luck

Let's say that you've established that you are an innately creative person, and you have even been able to develop a creative idea. You're set, right? Sadly, creativity alone may not be enough to ensure the success of your product or company. You also need to get the timing right. Keep in mind that sixdegrees. com had all the key features of a social network, but it launched back in 1997, at a time when the requisite technology to make full use of the site's features was far too expensive for the average user. By the time Facebook launched in 2004, however, the situation had changed drastically. Facebook was poised for growth on its launch because of certain major megatrends, including the following:

- The growth in use and abundance of affordable digital cameras

- The ubiquity of broadband

- The average user's increased comfort level with the Internet and growing willingness to disclose personal information on the Web

- The emergence of free open source software like MySQL and PHP, which made it possible for a student like Zuckerberg to create a world-class web site

If Zuckerberg had been born 10 years earlier and attended Harvard during the mid 1990s, Facebook might not have ever been invented. Entrepreneurs need to have a good sense for where technology is moving, what users want, and a bit of luck, and then jump on the opportunities those two factors present to them.

Simplicity and Focus

Make things as simple as possible, but not simpler.

—Albert Einstein

This quote appears on Zuckerberg's Facebook profile; it is the key to his product development philosophy. However, simplicity is not something that comes naturally to smart engineers. The temptation is to create products that boast loads of features—and not because engineers necessarily want to help end users—but just for the fun of creating interesting, new technologies.

Similarly, when a founder is building a new company, it is fairly common for her to flit from one idea to the next, trying to implement not just one but all of the latest, coolest, and most up-to-the-minute technologies. One day she might focus on mobile. The next day she wants to add a social networking component to her company. Then, after that, she's all abuzz about gamification. To a certain degree, this type of behavior makes sense, because it is a conditioned response to all the noise that is constantly floating around in the tech space. After all, if there are any constants when it comes to technology, it is that there will always be a new buzzword. Always. But take a minute to think about the one characteristic that each of today's top companies in tech, including LinkedIn, Zynga, and Pandora, have in common with one another. Give up? Their founders have all built billion-dollar enterprises by maintaining a laser focus on one product category.

For a young startup, straying from your focus is a terrible impulse that needs to be restrained. If you find that your venture has a tendency to veer off course when it comes to your product development efforts, a great way to regain the focus of your company, your cofounders, and your employees is to get in the habit of saying no to requests to add a little more of this and a little more of that. If you can't retain focus, your product will most likely wind up being too complex and messy to be helpful or of use to your end users. There's a phrase for the unfortunate habit of layering product feature upon product feature upon product feature: feature creep. Avoid it!

Idealistically, your product's purpose should be instantly clear to your end users; they should be able to identify immediately which of their key problems your product can solve. How was this the case with Facebook? Zuckerberg got the motivation to create the site from his frustration with the fact that the printed version of Harvard's facebook was always out of date. (Zuckerberg did not come up with the name Facebook on his own; it was first used by the university as the name for its directory of new students.) In Zuckerberg's eyes, it was a no-brainer to give Harvard's directory of students an online home on the Internet. However, Zuckerberg realized that his site should not just replicate Harvard's facebook on the Web. He knew that a superior approach to the site was to make it about sharing.

The first version of Facebook was actually fairly simple. It only took a couple weeks for Zuckerberg to bang out the code. The resulting welcome page was fairly bare bones in nature. In a sense, Zuckerberg was really one of the earliest practitioners of an approach called the lean startup, which is championed in Eric Ries's book *The Lean Startup* (Crown Business, 2011). Ries believes that success is about building a minimum viable product and then launching it to the world to obtain valuable feedback on it from users. After user feedback has been gathered, Ries asserts, it is then easier to evolve the product and gain traction in the appropriate market more quickly.

On their very first Facebook profile page, users could add the following information:

- E-mail address, name, gender, AOL Instant Messenger handle
- Relationship status
- Courses
- One photo
- Major and year enrolled
- Interests, including movies and books, and one quote

The earliest version of Facebook also let you leave public notes for your friends on their Facebook wall, but the concept was fairly basic and downright minimal compared with the Timeline that each Facebook user has access to today. You could also contact your friends using private messages. That was it—the whole functionality of the site. Not much, huh? But that was the point. Zuckerberg was focused on one thing and one thing alone: Solving a problem for students, which, in the case of Facebook, was helping students share information and connect with one another, perhaps for a study group or a date.

Let's face it; college is a big-time social experience that is predicated on building and exhibiting your social status. What better way of showing how popular you are than by displaying publicly how many friends you have? As a result, Facebook began to spread like wildfire. After a few months, students at other universities and colleges across the country were begging Zuckerberg to give their campus access to his social networking site.

When you look at Facebook's very first interface, you can see that it is clean and clearly understandable. Although the company periodically redesigned the web site, it did do so not to make Facebook cooler, but rather to make it even cleaner. Simplicity was a constant focus and, as it turned out, it was a major selling point. At the time Facebook launched, its only real social networking competitor was MySpace, whose design principles were the polar opposite of those at Facebook. Although Facebook used a one-size-fits-all approach to its overall site design and user profiles, MySpace was unwieldy, allowing users to customize their profile easily and, in doing so, creating a sense of chaos on the site. MySpace's customizable profiles would prove a huge stumbling block when it came to attracting older users who did not want to navigate through the somewhat psychedelic environment its younger first adopters had created.

Facebook's easy interface resulted in another advantage for end users: speed. All in all, users don't want to wait for the web sites they visit to load. Slow load times can quickly bring about the early demise of a web service, as was the case with Friendster. Because of its horrendous foundation, Friendster's pages loaded at a snail's space; the site could take more than a minute per page to load!

Since the launch of Facebook, Zuckerberg has continued to maintain his laser-sharp focus on simplicity. Take Facebook's Photos functionality, for example. Compared with rivals like Flickr, Photos seemed like a poor product. The resolution of uploaded images was low, users were not allowed to print photos off the site, and you could not even order the photos to be printed by a third party. In the end, however, these apparent shortcomings did not matter to end users. What mattered was that, in keeping with Zuckerberg's mission to enable online sharing, Photos allowed users to tag their friends in pictures in which they appeared. Photo tagging turned out to be yet another killer

Facebook feature, and in short order, Photos dominated the online photo-sharing space.

Elegant Design

Although a basic—even elementary—design was appropriate for Facebook, it is not necessarily the best approach for every startup. As with everything, the intricacy, look, and feel of your product's design depend entirely on its purpose. For example, if you want to create an app that allows users to "try on" digitally this season's latest fashions, your product almost assuredly requires a rich multimedia experience. Fashion is not the only product category for which a more robust design experience is appropriate. Take Fab.com, which bills itself as a flash-sales site for "discovering everyday design." When you navigate to Fab.com to search for potential purchases, you get the feeling that you have been included in a special experience. The site's layout and design just has a way of pulling you in to buying things.

An elegant design may also be necessary if the success of your app depends on establishing instant trust with your users. If your application deals with people's money, it is particularly important that you design it in a professional yet accessible manner, lest potential users take one look at your product and decide there's *no way* they would entrust their hard-earned cash to what appears to be an amateurish operation. How do you communicate that yours is a company to be trusted? Just look at Square. One glance at its interface tells you that Square is a company that cares about simplicity, professionalism, transparency, and quality. What's not to trust?

Engagement

Your product needs to be habit forming—something that your users come back to every day, a central hub where they gather to spend huge chunks of their time. In other words, your product must be engaging. No doubt, fostering engagement has been a hugely important priority for Facebook. Features like Facebook's News Feed and Photos were critical for creating user engagement—and for fending off rivals like MySpace. After all, the more time Internet users spend on Facebook, the less time they spend on rival social networking sites.

Facebook is not alone in the importance that it places on engagement. If you look at other top consumer Internet products, they are all habit forming as well. Anyone who has used Skype, YouTube, Zynga, Twitter, or Instagram knows how easy it is to lose an hour or two of your day to these web sites.

However, although it makes sense that users would return day after day (and often hour after hour) to hubs where they can access for free internationally integrated messaging, entertaining and informational videos, constant streams of international news and personal status updates, and visually appealing photos, there are certain categories of products in which user engagement is very difficult to achieve. Think, for example, about a theoretical site that caters to car buyers. Typical consumers purchase a car once every eight or nine years, so what reason would they have to return, time and time again— let alone day after day or hour after hour—to a site with the main purpose of helping users purchase a new car? The answer is: None. Car buyers only access the product site when they need it (which, in our example, is only once in a very long while), making it extremely expensive for this type of site to attract and retain users. Unless you come up with a unique business model— or an incredibly cheap way to attract and retain users—it is a good idea to stay away from product categories for which daily user engagement is difficult to achieve.

Convictions

If I had asked people what they wanted, they would have said faster horses.

—Henry Ford

All great product developers know that consumers do not know that they want or need a given product until they start using it. However, actually developing a product that consumers don't know that they need is no easy feat! To make matters worse, consumers tend to be resistant to change, so it's extremely challenging to convince them to start using your new product in the first place. Regardless, few tasks are more crucial to a company's success than creating a product that consumers grow to love and rely on in their day-to-day lives.

When Zuckerberg first came up with the idea for News Feed, it made a lot of sense to redesign Facebook in such a way that users could view instantaneously what their friends were up to on logging on to the site. However, when the feature was launched, there was a huge uproar from users, who said that the redesign made Facebook feel too cluttered. Users also voiced concerns about privacy, even though News Feed did not provide any extra information on users than was already available on the site. The only difference was News Feed made information that once required a concerted search easily accessible in one central hub. But users, of course, were frustrated and uploaded a constant stream of messages to the tune of "I feel violated" and "You've ruined my life."

What would a typical CEO do if confronted by this same type of situation? Probably back off and kill the new feature. Yet had Zuckerberg done away with News Feed, Facebook would likely not have turned into the megaphenomenon it is today. Zuckerberg knew that users would eventually come to understand the value of News Feed because it was central to the mission of Facebook: to improve users' ability to connect and share with one another. Within a few weeks of News Feed's launch, the furor died down and News Feed became a must-have component of Facebook!

There are, of course, risks to the approach Zuckerberg took with News Feed. A classic example is Digg. Founded in 2004, Digg was one of the pioneers in social media and gained instant traction. Over time, Digg was able to create a loyal user base that was interested in ranking the top stories of the day. This would change, though, in 2010, when the company underwent a major site redesign. As was the case with Facebook, users were outraged and began to flee to rivals like Twitter, but Digg remained committed to its new design and would not back down. In the end, the redesign was catastrophic, because it caused Digg's user base to dwindle quickly.

So why did Digg waste away in the same type of situation in which Facebook thrived? Digg's problem was that the site's redesign really did not do much for its core mission. If anything, the redesign was mostly a reaction to emerging sites like Facebook and Twitter. Digg essentially wanted to copy these sites' popular features, despite the fact that its users were passionately saying that they wanted Digg to be Digg and not some other type of service. Had the site gone back to its original approach or rolled back many of the needless features it added in the redesign, the disaster could have been averted. Loyal users tolerate mistakes, but not if the core focus of the site changes drastically.

Fun Stuff

Some products can be too focused on solving problems and, as a result, lack an element of fun. Fun features—even if they do not enhance your product's usability—can, in and of themselves, lead to added user engagement. In the case of Facebook, Zuckerberg decided to add one particular feature, known as the poke, purely and simply for fun. Says Zuckerberg, "When we created the poke, we thought it would be cool to have a feature without any specific purpose. People interpret the poke in many different ways, and we encourage you to come up with your own meanings."[2]

---

[2] Dave Copeland, "Just Try Poking Someone Now," *The Daily Dot*, September 20, 2011, www.dailydot.com/news/facebook-poke-hidden/.

And people have! People use Facebook's poke function for any number of reasons, whether they are using it to meet new people, to flirt with a friend, or to say hello in a fun and playful way. Regardless of how or why it is used, the poke lends Facebook an added layer of character, frivolity, and approachability, all of which are qualities from which any startup can benefit.

Groupon is another example of a company who has used fun—specifically humor—to set itself apart from its hundreds of competitors. The company sends out daily e-mail messages to encourage users to keep on clicking and buying. Groupon often sends funny offer descriptions, such as the following for a horse ride: "Without horses," the copywriter notes, "polo shirts would be branded with monkeys and Paul Revere would have been forced to ride on a Segway. Celebrate our hoofed counterparts with today's Groupon."[3] Given the wit, skill, and diversity of offer descriptions that find their way into users' inbox each day, it should come as no surprise that Groupon has more than 400 copywriters on staff, which is more than some of the world's brand organizations.

A Platform

For technology companies, developing a platform that becomes a global standard is the equivalent of finding the Holy Grail. In the early days of Microsoft's history, Bill Gates (who actually was the first person to come up with the concept of *platform*) was approached by IBM, who wanted him to help them with their personal computer (PC) project. Gates realized that if he could develop an operating system that could run on almost any IBM-compatible computer, Microsoft stood a good chance of owning the rights to the world's standard-issue operating system. In response, Gates created MS-DOS, and, as he had predicted, the operating system was wildly successful and became the operating system that was bundled for use on all PCs. In fact, the concept of developing a standard-issue platform was so lucrative for Gates and Microsoft that he applied it to Windows and the Office Suite. As a result, even though other players have competed fiercely against these product lines, Microsoft still has huge market shares in the computing and software spaces—even after several decades. Not many tech companies can claim the same.

Like Gates, Zuckerberg realized the importance of developing something bigger than a single-focused software program or web site, which is why he created Facebook with the end goal of turning it into a platform or even a utility. In essence, Zuckerberg wanted Facebook to be the core for all of its

---

[3] David Streitfeld, "Funny or Die: Groupon's Fate Hinges on Words," *The New York Times*, May 28, 2011, www.nytimes.com/2011/05/29/business/29groupon.html?pagewanted=all.

users' social activities. To turn this goal into a reality, Zuckerberg took some crucial steps. One was to allow third parties to create apps on Facebook, a decision that set the stage for the current Facebook ecosystem and led to the creation of megacompanies like Zynga. Another important step Zuckerberg took was to develop Facebook Connect, which makes it possible for other web sites to register new users via Facebook's social login.

If you think your company has a platform opportunity, you need to take some important steps. It is critical that you devote an immense amount of resources to providing support services, which entails more than just giving developers access to code and modules. You need to create a developers' program that has clear-cut terms, training programs, and frequent updates. You should also hold ongoing conferences and meetings to encourage new developer members to join your platform.

Creating a platform involves a lot of work, so make sure you're ready to anticipate the potential questions and the possible problems that developers may encounter when using your utility before you launch your platform. If your company is in its early stages, think about waiting to create and launch a platform until your user base has reached critical mass and can grab the attention of potential developers. Consider that Facebook waited 3 years before launching its own program; and even with the wait, the platform still had many glitches in its early days.

Reactive Product Design

When a company introduces a new feature or product to ward off the threat of encroachment from a rival, it is engaging in reactive product design. However, fighting rivals on a feature-by-feature basis can harm the long-term prospects of your company. As discussed earlier in this chapter, adding new features just for the sake of keeping up with the Joneses is likely to create confusion and undue complexity for your users. It can also cause you to veer away from your company's mission.

Even the best companies, Facebook included, can be found guilty of reactive product design and, generally speaking, it does not work out for them. For example, when the check-in service Foursquare became popular, Facebook launched its Places feature, but the service was a flop and was discontinued in short order. Then, in April 2011, Facebook launched Deals, which looked a lot like Groupon. The service was piloted in five cities but got little traction and it was eventually canceled as well.

This is not to say that it is wrong to experiment with adding new features from time to time. Keep in mind that even though Facebook's Subscribe feature—which pushes to your News Feed the public updates of users to which you decide to subscribe—looks a lot like Twitter, the service was a good idea and is consistent with Zuckerberg's mission. So, be conscientious when you are thinking about adding a new feature and ask yourself: Am I doing this because it's good for my users or because I don't want to be left behind? If you can't genuinely say that the feature will benefit your users, spare yourself the hassle and forget about it.

Mobile First

There's little doubt that mobile is a megatrend and represents a huge opportunity for tech startups. The key driver in mobile is the supergrowth in smartphones, especially in devices running Apple's iOS and Google's Android. Table 3-1 includes just a few data points regarding the anticipated growth in mobile from 2011 to 2016. As you can see, the figures are staggering.

Table 3-1. Anticipated Growth in Mobile Devices from 2011 to 2016

Mobile Trends	Forecast
Number of smartphones shipped	494 million in 2011, 1.16 billion by 2016[4]
Number of tablets shipped	107.4 million in 2012, 222.1 million by 2016[5]
Downloads of mobile apps	31 billion in 2011, 66 billion by 2016[6]
Mobile entertainment revenues	$36 billion in 2011, $65 billion by 2016[7]

Source: IDC, Informa Telecoms, and Media, Gartner.

Smartphones and tablets are becoming an integral part of the daily lives of many consumers who are using these highly habit-forming devices to check

---

[4] Jeff Blagdon, "IDC Forecasts 1.16 Billion Smartphones Shipped Annually by 2016 ," The Verge, March 29, 2012, theverge.com/2012/3/29/2910399/idc-smartphone-computer-tablet-sales-2011.
[5] Dan Graziano, "IDC Ups Tablet Estimates, Expects Shipments to Reach 222.1 Million by 2016," BGR, Jun2 15, 2012, www.bgr.com/2012/06/15/apple-ipad-android-tablet-shipments/.
[6] Jason Ankeny, "Forecast: Consumers Will Download 66B Mobile Apps Annually by 2016," Fierce Mobile Content, April 5, 2012, www.fiercemobilecontent.com/story/forecast-consumers-will-download-66b-mobile-apps-annually-2016/2012-04-05.
[7] Jeff Blagdon, "Mobile Entertainment Revenues to Eclipse $65B in 2016," Fierce Mobile Content, March 29, 2012, www.fiercemobilecontent.com/story/forecast-mobile-entertainment-revenues-eclipse-65b-2016/2012-06-13.

out the news, shop, get directions, listen to music, and play games. Have you noticed how many people walk and drive while looking down at their smartphones?

Mobile users are also increasingly using their devices for social networking, so it should come as no surprise that mobile usage on Facebook has surged. By the first quarter of 2012, the site had more than 500 million monthly active users for its mobile products.

However, Facebook has struggled with developing mobile products, which thus far have tended to be relatively slow and are packed with too many features. Why is Facebook still struggling with these issues? It could be because Facebook's DNA is that of a Web-based company that focuses on users' desktop experience. Creating an engaging interface for the mobile environment is a whole different ballgame. Success in mobile is not a matter of just slapping a Web app on a mobile device; rather, you have to understand how to create a strong mobile experience for your users.

It should not be a surprise, then, that Facebook plunked down $1 billion for Instagram, a fast-growing mobile photo app that had begun to threaten Photos, a key component of Facebook's business. Instagram, which is an example of a company with a primary focus on the development of its mobile app (also known as a mobile-first company), understands that when it comes to mobile, simplicity is even more important than it is with desktop apps. When Kevin Systrom and Michel Krieger created Instagram, they first brainstormed all the problems they had with existing mobile photo-sharing apps—and there were many. From there, they wanted to solve three of the most frustrating problems they could come up with:

1. Mobile photos don't look so good. They often seemed to be washed out, most likely because of poor lighting. People wanted better quality pictures from their phones without having to be a professional photographer.

2. The uploading process for pictures was too long.

3. It was not easy to share photos across multiple social networks like Facebook and Twitter.

Once Systrom and Krieger had narrowed their focus and identified only the most pressing problems with mobile photo sharing, it was much easier to come up with the solutions to these problems. (Funny enough, it usually is harder to find the problems with an existing structure, not the solutions!) To address problem number one—picture quality—they created filters that made the pictures look beautiful and almost as if they were retro 1970s photos. As for problem number two—upload speed—the duo built the app so it would process the upload while users were doing other things on the app, like filling out photo captions. To improve problem number three, they simply sought to understand and integrate more completely the various platforms into their app.

Instagram launched on October 6, 2010, and it was a runaway hit. By the end of the year, it had reached 1 million registered users. In April 2012, when Facebook agreed to buy the company, it had increased its head count to 30 million registered users. Although Instagram's success is undoubtedly remarkable, it is even more so when you consider that there are hundreds of thousands of mobile apps available for download, making it extremely difficult for any one app to stand out from the rest of the crowd.

If you're intent on breaking out in the mobile app arena, there are some best practices to keep in mind. Perhaps the most important is to enter into an app category that is known to be habit forming, like photo and video sharing or games, to hook your users and keep them coming back to engage with your app again and again. Speaking of categories, if your app doesn't fit neatly into one of the available categories on the app store, try to reposition it so that it does. Otherwise, marketing your app may prove extremely difficult. Last, although your app need not be overly simplistic, it should focus on a single function. If you include too many pages, too many features, too much complexity, you will most likely lose users' interest; so, make your app instantly easy to understand and use. Often, this means sticking to the standards of your chosen app development program, which—as an added bonus—should make it easier for your app to sail through the approval process!

Stealth Startup

Although the concept of a *stealth startup*—a startup that is working on its product in secret—sounds cool and may work for some types of businesses, such as high-end corporate networking technologies, it is often a bad idea for companies that are developing consumer Internet and mobile apps. After all, it is crucial to get user feedback on your product early on. Instagram's Systrom calls the process of beta testing your product the "bar exam," which consists of going to a bar and showing people your app. By observing their reactions, you can gain some valuable insights about your product.

Beta testing proved critical for Instagram. Its first mobile app, Burbn, allowed users to check in to different places, but when they saw that it wasn't gaining much traction in the marketplace, Systrom and Krieger set out to find out why. After talking to their users about Burbn's features, Systrom and Krieger realized a common theme kept recurring in their conversations with users: The app's photo-sharing feature was quite popular. The good businessmen that they are, Systrom and Krieger decided to abandon Burbn and focus on developing their photo-sharing feature into a full-blown app; as a result, Instagram was born.

In essence, Systrom and Krieger pivoted, which is another word for when a company abandons its original product and moves into another category. Not long ago, pivot would have been another word for failure, but in today's world, in which the costs of starting a business are much lower, it is possible for a company to make a radical shift in its product strategy or business model. In fact, investors have even come to expect these types of moves. Instagram is not the only company to arise from a successful pivot. Table 3-2 outlines a few other notable pivots of which you might not be aware.

Table 3-2. Examples of Company Pivoting

Company	Pivot
Groupon	The site was originally called *ThePoint* and was built to help organize fund-raisers. It bombed, but the company's founder, Andrew Mason, saw that the platform could be a great way to revolutionize the coupon business.
OMGPOP	The site started as a dating site called *Iminlikewithyou* (terrible name, huh?). The company then focused on gaming and created Draw Something. Zynga bought the company for $180 million.
Fab.com	Starting as a gay social network, Fab.com got little traffic, so the founders pivoted and turned it into a flash site for apparel and home goods.

Keep in mind that after a pivot, it is important to maintain an insane amount of focus on your product when you develop something that strikes a chord with users. Constant pivoting is a strategy that is likely to go nowhere—and your investors will likely go elsewhere.

Physical World

For tech entrepreneurs, it is easy to become a slave to the virtual world. But doing so can limit your venture. Hey, people like playing in the real world, too. Look at the kids (and the adults!) who have tons of fun at Disneyland. Or how about a wine tasting tour in Napa? Or a great vacation to, say, Antarctica?

When brainstorming a new business concept, don't forget to keep the real world in mind, because companies that meld elements of the virtual and real worlds are already gaining traction in the marketplace. Take Birchbox, for example. The founders, Katia Beauchamp and Hayley Barna, got the inspiration for their company while they were students at Harvard Business School. They wanted to have a way to access a selection of great beauty products, but because of their demanding work schedules and studies, they did not have the time to source the products themselves. Birchbox solves that problem. For $10 a month, members receive a box filled with samples of beauty products based upon their preselected interests. All in all, Birchbox has turned into a great experience for its members and the beauty companies that supply the samples. The service has grown at a rapid pace. Originally, cosmetic companies were finding it difficult to leverage Internet technology to market and sell their products, because it is important for consumers to see, smell, and use their products before making a purchasing decision. With Birchbox, this problem is solved.

In this chapter, we've seen how success in product development is really the result of solving one or two big problems that your customers have. How do you do that? Think about some of the problems that have frustrated you personally and then set out to solve them for others. It's important to understand, though, that it is not a good idea to spend too much time building your solutions. The real value is in getting your product to market quickly so that you can start receiving valuable feedback from your early adopters. In a way, a good product is never really completed; it is always evolving. In the next chapter, we take a look at a hot topic—funding. Even if your product takes off, you still need outside capital to make sure it is built to last.

Raising Capital

The lack of money is the root of all evil.

—Mark Twain

In a market where speed is critical, outside funding allows young companies to move faster than they otherwise could if they had to rely only on their own revenues to fund product development. Sure, receiving outside funding means you'll have to give up some of your company's equity, but over time, the early sting you might feel when sacrificing a percentage of your shares to get your company up off the ground and running will diminish. If you create a valuable company, the initial dilution of your shares is worth it in the end. Even wealthy entrepreneurs often raise capital. What better way is there to determine whether something you have created is valuable than finding someone who is willing to write a check to fund it?

As we saw in Chapter 2, Mark Zuckerberg made some major blunders with his initial attempts at seed funding Facebook. His original investor, Eduardo Saverin, ultimately froze the company's bank account! However, Zuckerberg learned from the experience and later wound up raising $2 billion from private investors in an effort that proved critical to Facebook's success. But how, exactly, do you go about securing seed funding? Do you just call up a wealthy friend and ask for an infusion of cash? In this chapter, we take a look at the different types of investors you might want to approach, the cycles of funding, and some helpful tips on timing your funding efforts.

Start up Lite

The costs of starting up a company have declined substantially during the past few years, at least for those in the web and mobile app spaces. After all, most mobile or web products can be hosted, launched, and distributed easily and inexpensively on cloud services such as Amazon Web Services, thereby eliminating the hassle and potential expense of self-distribution. You can start easily with a small amount of storage and bandwidth, and, as your business begins to grow, pay for additional capacity as the need arises. This pay-as-you-go approach is the hallmark of cloud computing and makes life much easier for the startup entrepreneur.

So, for the most part, then, the "cost" of a tech startup is the time it takes for the team to code the product. Your out-of-pocket expenses will likely be well under $25,000, much of which will go toward your company's legal fees. This is in stark contrast to the dot-com boom of the 1990s, when it took $5 million to $10 million just to obtain vital components of tech infrastructure, such as Oracle databases, licenses to servers, and hardware. All of this is to say that although you may think you need to raise millions of dollars to launch and develop your product successfully, odds are that you will need far less capital than you might expect.

If your product gains momentum, then you are in a much better position to pique the interest of investors whose cash infusions will help you scale your company, which means to accelerate the growth rate. You should also be able to get a better valuation on whatever funding deal you strike with them. Don't think that you have to draft an executive summary or a business plan when you are still in the early stages of developing your product to draw in investors. Rather, focus on speed and on developing some critical features that will solve your customers' problems. In many cases, success is the by-product of pursuing a project that solves a specific problem you have. As was mentioned in Chapter 3, Zuckerberg created Facebook because he wanted a better way to connect with his school friends, and things turned out pretty well for him.

Know the Types of Investors That Are Out There

If your product is getting traction in the marketplace, then the time has come to seek out investors. Keep in mind that there are many types of investors you can approach, each of which specializes in a specific phase of the financing cycle of a new company. Read on to learn about the main players.

Angels and Superangels

Angel investors are those who invest their own money in early-stage ventures. For the most part, angels are wealthy and meet the U.S. Securities and

Exchange Commission's requirements to act as accredited investors. In addition, many angels have started their own companies or are executives; so, as an added bonus, they often bring incredibly valuable business experience to a venture. Don't be alarmed if you encounter angels who wish to make their investment in your company through a legal structure, such as a trust or an LLC. Angels use such structures because they lower taxes and provide liability protection, not because they're trying to scam you.

You may also talk to so-called *superangels*, or high-profile entrepreneurs, who carry a lot of clout within the startup community and become serial investors in early-stage ventures. It's not unheard of for superangels to invest upward of $1 million in the ventures they decide to seed. In many cases, superangels invest money on behalf of other angel investors by creating a micro venture capital fund. Some examples include Jeff Clavier's SofTechVC and Chris Sacca's Lowercase Capital.

Venture Capitalists

Although venture capital is thought of as a fairly new industry, its roots go all the way back to the 1940s, and it started gaining momentum as early as the late 1970s, when VCs funded breakout companies such as Genentech and Apple (keep in mind that VC is a broad term and refers to both a firm and the partners). It was during this time that some of today's most iconic VC firms, such as Kleiner Perkins and Sequoia, got their start.

Many of these operators set up their offices along Sand Hill Road in Menlo Park, California, which to this day remains the epicenter of venture capital. It is a boon to budding entrepreneurs that Sand Hill Road runs along Interstate 280, which connects San Jose and San Francisco, and is in close proximity to Stanford University. Furthermore, because so many firms are concentrated in such a small area, it is relatively easy and inexpensive, travelwise, to pitch to VCs. An entrepreneur can easily pitch to four or five VCs in a single day!

Unlike angels and superangels, VCs invest money on behalf of their investors, who are known as *limited partners* and include institutions, such as endowments, insurance companies, and pensions, as well as wealthy individual investors (usually, former entrepreneurs). In this respect, a VC is essentially a money manager; any given firm has several partners that seek out investment opportunities, structure investments, and provide follow-on funding.

Every few years, a VC firm will invite several of the firm's investors to combine their capital into one large fund to invest in an array of startup companies. Each fund that a VC firm creates lasts for 10 to 12 years, which, ideally, is just enough time for the firm to sell all its equity stakes in its portfolio companies. However, because it is now taking much longer for companies to go public—

in part because founders want to retain more control over their ventures, but also because it is very expensive to pull off an IPO—more and more VCs are extending their funds' lifetimes.

The partners in a venture fund generate income from two sources. First, they charge a management fee, which can range from 1.5% to 2.5%, and is based on the size of the assets in the fund and is paid every year until the fund is closed down. For the most part, the management fee is meant to help the partners with their overhead costs. For a large fund, however—say, $1 billion or more—management fees can turn into lucrative compensation for the partners.

The second way in which the partners of a venture fund are compensated is via carried interest, also known as carry, which generally amounts to 20% to 25% of the profits from the fund and is paid out as a performance incentive. Again, a partner working at a large fund can command substantial fees from carried interest. For example, suppose a VC fund generates $1 billion in profits. In this case, the fund's partners will divvy up $200 million to $250 million, which explains why many VCs drive fancy cars and have multiple homes.

The VC game, however, isn't exactly a surefire way to rake in heaps of money. It can be brutal. Because the majority of investments a VC makes will be wipeouts, firms need to invest in ventures that can ultimately become franchise companies, such as Facebook. The goal is that these huge winners will more than compensate for the many losers in a VC's portfolio. Unfortunately, however, this isn't always the case. Although tier 1 operators have been able to generate standout returns in recent years, the majority of firms have posted lackluster returns since 2000. As a result, there has been substantial attrition in the number of VC firms in operation throughout the years.

Strategic Investors

As companies grow larger, it can become more difficult for them to innovate, despite how essential it is for them to do so. Often, in lieu of hiring a chief innovation officer or trying to innovate from within, an established company makes what are known as *strategic investments* in early-stage ventures with the goal of gaining valuable insights into new technologies or markets. Strategic investments can even be used as a way to stifle the competition. For example, a key reason that Microsoft invested in Facebook was to prevent Google from taking a stake in the company; the investment documents that Microsoft drew up specifically prohibited Facebook from taking money from the search engine giant. However, Microsoft received other important benefits when it invested in Facebook. As part of the deal, Microsoft was given the green light to sell banner ads on Facebook outside the United States, splitting the revenue with the young startup. It also gave Microsoft the opportunity to learn the nuances of social networking. Oh, and the investment turned out to be a big gainer.

So, why should a startup take money from a strategic investor? One reason is that valuation negotiations with strategic investors are usually straightforward, because strategic investors in general are looking for company synergies and not necessarily a substantial monetary return on investment. A strategic investment can also be a validator and vote of confidence for a young company, which can make it easier for the startup to attract new customers. Last, a startup can leverage its strategic investor's infrastructure and distribution channels, potentially leading to wider exposure and more opportunities for growth. For a startup, it is important to establish specific deliverables—in other words, benefits that the strategic investor will provide, such as introductions or promotion assistance—when brokering a deal with a strategic investor to maximize the value received from the investment.

No doubt, there are downsides to strategic investment, the most notable of which is exposing you to the need to navigate through corporate bureaucracy. It might be agonizingly slow to get much feedback or traction from your strategic investor; therefore, try to avoid giving your strategic investor a board seat or veto rights on major decisions. You should also try to avoid negotiating any exclusive partnerships with your strategic investor because these can ultimately limit your company's growth potential.

Venture Lenders

To avoid issuing too many shares and running the risk of diluting their stock, which has the potential to wind up in the wrong hands, many startups seek out debt financing, which involves borrowing money. This may seem like a strange strategy for an early-stage company, but debt financing is actually a viable option for new ventures, thanks to recent developments in startup funding.

During the past decade, a variety of top venture lenders have emerged whose financing provides startups with working capital and helps them buy equipment or meet their short-term needs. If you think only a desperate or flailing startup would seek out venture lenders, think again; Facebook actually borrowed money from venture lenders, such as WTI and TriplePoint Capital, as recently as 2009, when the company's credibility and worth were already well established.

Prior to signing a debt-financing deal with a startup, venture lenders establish the term of the loan, which usually ranges from 2 to 4 years. Then, in return for their willingness to front the startup working capital, the venture lenders gain competitive interest on the loan—perhaps 5% to 7%. However, venture lenders also want to acquire some equity in the startup as a condition of the loan. As a result, the startup issues its venture lender an agreed-on number of shares through a warrant, which is similar to a stock option in that it gives the investor the right to buy shares at a fixed price for up to 10 years. The worth of the warrant is usually expressed as a percentage of the overall amount of financing the venture lender provides. For example, if a company borrows $1 million from a venture lender and the warrant coverage is 10%, then the warrant allows the lender to buy $100,000 of common stock. For the most part, venture lenders only provide debt financing to startups that are backed by venture capital, because doing so provides some level of safety for the loan.

Late-Stage Funders

Private equity funds, hedge funds, and mutual funds, from time to time, provide late-stage funding for startups they deem to be promising. By investing in more mature companies, late-stage funders have the opportunity to gain strong returns from their investments, but with a significantly lower level of risk because the startups that survive to this later point have most likely achieved impressive sales and established their worth in the marketplace. On the flip side, for the company that is seeking it, late-stage funding is usually a way to generate secondary sales and to allow its existing shareholders—whether they are investors or employees—to sell some of their holdings to these funds. It is also a way to infuse liquidity into the startup without having to file for an IPO, which can be expensive and disruptive to the startup's operations.

Yuri Milner, who operates Digital Sky Technologies (DST), was one of the first innovators in late-stage funding—and an unlikely one, at that. Born in Russia, he went to school at Wharton and then returned home to buy a macaroni factory, which turned out to be a tremendous cash cow. When the dot-com bust hit in 2001, Milner purchased the e-mail service Mail.ru for $100 million and, within a few years, it became the No. 2 Internet company in Russia. Flush with cash, Milner then contacted Facebook and said he wanted to buy shares in the company. His timing was perfect; when he got in touch with Facebook, the world economy was still in the throes of the financial crisis of 2008, making his offer extremely attractive to Facebook. The company eventually agreed to the deal, and DST invested $200 million in the social networking giant while taking a "hands-off" approach to the investment. In a sense, DST's late-stage investment in Facebook was almost like an IPO, because the investment gave the firm no ultimate control over the site. Since then, Milner has made late-stage investment plays in other well-known companies such as Twitter, Spotify, Zynga, Groupon, and Airbnb.

Late-stage funding has become a common part of the startup landscape. These investments make it possible for founders to defer filing an IPO and provide liquidity to early investors and employees. The funding also provides substantial resources to help accelerate a venture's growth and position it to dominate new markets. However, it isn't exactly easy to attract the interest of late-stage investors. A company must have the potential to become a franchise player—complete with a global brand and substantial barriers to entry, such as with its customer base, technology, and distribution—before late-stage investors give it a second glance. The good news, though, is that such attributes are obvious in the marketplace and late-stage funders often approach worthy companies to inquire about making an investment.

Understand the Stages of Investing

In general, a startup goes through four different types of rounds of financing: seed, angel, venture capital, and IPO. Let's take a look at each one in detail.

Seed Funding

Seed funding, which is often a company's first round of funding and generally involves fairly small amounts of capital, from perhaps $1,000 to $100,000, allows a startup's cofounders to test their hypothetical product. This testing usually entails creating a beta version of their product and seeing whether it gains any traction with potential investors, who may include the company's founders, friends, family, and maybe angel investors. One of the more popular sources of seed funding is through the use of the founders' personal credit cards, which is exactly how Facebook survived the first year of its existence. However, investments can also be drummed up creatively, such as when the founders of Box financed the company with $20,000 they made from playing online poker!

Generally speaking, for most startups the seed stage is a mess. Founders who are enmeshed in the seed funding stage of their company's development tend to give little thought to legal matters or business formalities. They probably will have issues with a lack of communication, as well. Facebook suffered from these classic problems, too. Like many first-time entrepreneurs, Zuckerberg had no experience with business and legal matters when he first launched Facebook, but this is no excuse for you to do the same. It does not take much work to build a solid foundation of business and legal knowledge. As we talked about in Chapter 2, there are some legal moves, such as incorporating a C-Corp in Delaware, protecting your intellectual property, and exercising an 83(b) election, you can make to position your startup for success. Sure, concerning yourself with the business and legal minutiae of starting up a company isn't fun and may delay your speed a bit, but it will be well worth the effort in the end.

Angel Funding

Compared with the seed funding stage, angel rounds of financing typically involve much larger investments, which can range in size from $100,000 to $1,000,000. In the case of Facebook, Zuckerberg raised $600,000 in its first angel round, including $500,000 from Peter Thiel and $40,000 from both Reid Hoffman and Mark Pincus. The remaining $20,000 was contributed by several other individuals.

So, how do you find angels? Doing so takes a lot of work and is certainly not the easiest endeavor in the world, but the following sections provide several helpful strategies to make your search easier.

Angel Networks

Angel networks are organized groups of angel investors consisting of anywhere from 20 to 100 members that meet up about once a month to look at new startups in which to invest. When angel networks decide to strike a deal with a startup, the investment amounts can be large—say, more than $1 million.

There are several reputable angel groups in many large cities across America and they usually have web sites that detail the process by which they select startups for investment funding. However, angel networks typically become aware of your company because you either get a personal introduction to a member or you submit an executive summary for the network to review. If your deal meets the network's initial criteria, you'll be invited to make a presentation to the group, which—heads up—may be quite small. Some angel networks require you to pay a fee before presenting to the group, but I'd avoid networks with this type of requirement. After all, the best investors want to find early-stage investment opportunities, not draw in additional income from cash-strapped entrepreneurs.

Assuming your presentation to the angel network goes well, a member of the group acts as the "champion of the deal," typically ushers you through the rest of the angel round of financing, helping you target other potential investors and improving your pitch to investors. Your deal champion also conducts due diligence on your venture by performing reference checks and reviewing your intellectual property. Last, the angel network draws up a term sheet, which looks similar to those used during venture rounds of financing, and includes a bulleted list that outlines the terms and conditions of your business agreement with the group. For more on term sheets, check out Chapter 6.

AngelList.com

AngelList.com has become the key portal for matching startups with angel investors, and its members include such entrepreneurial heavyweights as Reid Hoffman, Fred Wilson, Brad Feld, Dave Morin, Chris Sacca, and Marc Andreessen, to name only a few. When you join AngelList, you are asked to create a profile for your company that details basic information about your company, describes why you are joining the site, and outlines who your core team members are. You are also asked to list a "referrer," who, ideally, is a well-known entrepreneur or angel investor who is willing to provide some credibility—and hopefully funding—to your venture. If your referrer is not willing to invest in your company, well, you better be prepared for when the other angels on the web site ask why. Of course, you also should make sure that your referrer knows that you're listing him as such on the site!

After you're all signed up, angels can follow your company and make comments on your business and its progress (which can be extremely helpful). For this reason, it is important that you upload a rock-solid executive summary and investor deck to your profile, which is the slide presentation. You should also take advantage of any visual collateral your team has developed, such as screen shots or video demos, because all these items can grab the attention of potential investors. Furthermore, make sure that you include the specific amount of funding you want to raise, as well as your company's valuation, and it certainly doesn't hurt to mention the type of security, such as convertible debt or common stock, that you will issue investors in return for their investment.

To get your company off on the right foot, it helps first to contact angels you already know and ask them for introductions to other angels on the site. Investor leads should start materializing in no time, but make sure that you are quick to respond to investor interest as much as possible, lest potential investors go cold and lose interest in your venture, which can happen easily. Often, founders ask potential investors if they want to schedule an online video chat, which can be a time-efficient, high-impact way to meet interested angels and to continue building your company's momentum. If it turns out that a contact made through the site does not result in an investment, you may find that the introduction is beneficial nonetheless if that angel becomes a valuable advisor to your company.

Old-Fashioned Networking

In all seriousness, if you want to raise money from angels—or VCs, for that matter—you need to be in close proximity to them, so move to Silicon Valley or New York City or perhaps even Los Angeles. All these places have tech ecosystems and are filled with angel investors who understand how startups work and, more important, have the funds to finance your business. Try to frequent the restaurants and bars where these investors are regulars. However, if you're looking for a more authentic environment in which to meet potential angels, you can also attend investor and tech conferences, because these types of gatherings are a favorite haunt of investors. Over time, you'll start to get to know some of the major players in the world of angel investing.

Another good, old-fashioned networking possibility is to find an advisor who has gone through the startup funding experience himself. Zuckerberg's funding advisor was Sean Parker, an entrepreneur who had developed extensive contacts in Silicon Valley while he was in his mid 20s and who made the necessary contacts to arrange for Facebook's angel round of funding. Last, if you're truly serious about starting up your own business, you can gain an enormous amount of experience and contacts by first working at a hot startup or top tech company, such as Facebook or Google. If you choose to go this route, you may not only get to know investors but also to develop crucial relationships with possible cofounders and engineers. Take Ben Silbermann, for example. After first working at Google as a product manager, Silbermann went on to cofound Pinterest in 2010. The site is now the No. 3 social network in the United States.

Accelerators

Similar to angel groups but often boasting their own office space for the ventures they decide to back, accelerators tend to provide ongoing advice and mentorship to fledgling startups, not to mention all-important seed funding. Some of today's top startup accelerators include YCombinator and Techstars, and these programs typically provide seed funding in an amount ranging from $50,000 to $200,000, which really is enough for a small team to develop a proof of concept and determine whether it has enough promise to go on to receive venture funding. Some notable startups that were accepted and funded by accelerators include Instagram, Dropbox, and Airbnb.

Crowdfunding

Crowdfunding involves leveraging a public web site to raise funds for a venture from the public. Until the passage of the Jumpstart Our Business Startups (JOBS) Act in early 2012, it was illegal for business ventures to seek equity funding via crowdsourcing. Now that the act has been signed into law, however, startups can fund their operations using one of three types of models:

1. *Peer-to-peer lending:* If you have a good credit score, peer-to-peer lending sites will help you borrow money from a number

lenders, each of whom may contribute $100 or so to your cause. Although peer-to-peer lending is actually a well-developed approach to crowdfunding, the maximum amount that most sites allow you to borrow is usually around $25,000.

2.   *Donation:* With donation-based crowdfunding sites, people contribute a small amount of money to your project in return for a small perk, such as being named in the credits of your movie or receiving a t-shirt. A big player in this market is Kickstarter.

3.   *Prepurchase and equity:* When you use the prepurchase model to fund your venture, your funders receive your product for free in exchange for their early-stage investment. Although initially the prepurchase model was frequented by those who were selling a physical product, such as a cool shoe or a new-fangled mobile device, the JOBS Act has made it possible for companies to issue stock in return for their funders' invest-ment, with a limit of $1 million in aggregate funding per year. For example, suppose you have already raised $200,000 in funding for your venture from a couple of friends. In this case, the JOBS Act only entitles you to raise an additional $800,000 from a crowdfunding site.

Since the adoption of the JOBS Act, there has been a proliferation of crowdfunding sites with the main purpose of helping companies gather the necessary documents for their funding efforts and seeking out potential investors. In exchange for their services, these sites charge a fee to the ventures that use them, which usually amounts to a percentage of the total funds raised. Because this industry is in its early stages, there are no clear-cut standards yet regarding the sites' fee levels; however, they will probably round out to at least 10% of the total funds raised.

According to the stipulations of the JOBS Act, investors who make less than $100,000 per year can make crowdfunding investments in an amount that is the greater of $2,000 or 5% of their income or net worth each year. For those over this threshold, the limit is the greater of $100,000 or 10% of their income or net worth each year. On the other side of the equation, if a company raises less than $100,000 using crowdfunding, its CEO must certify that the company's income tax returns and financial statements are true and complete. If it raises from $100,000 to $500,000 using crowdfunding, a certified public accounting firm must vouch for its financials. If it raises more than $500,000 using crowdfunding, it is subjected to an official audit.

Be wary. Many crowdfunding operators are small and may not necessarily be legitimate. When it comes to companies that handle investor money, there is always the temptation for fraud, so before using a crowdfunding site, look at the backgrounds of the site's principals. If there is even a hint of a shady past, do not partake of the site's services. At all times, focus on using those crowdfunding sites that have broker–dealer licenses, which is an indication that they can sell securities to the public legally.

Even if you find a reputable site, I still caution that crowdfunding is not a particularly good route to take for ventures seeking early-stage funding. Interestingly enough, receiving upfront crowdfunding money could make it more difficult to obtain follow-on investment from VCs later on. Why? When you crowdfund your venture, you are giving scores of individual investors early access to your shares and, generally speaking, VCs are reluctant to jump in on a deal with baggage that includes many small investors who, collectively, can cause a litany of administrative headaches. If anything, VCs try to find ways to buy off smaller, crowdfunding investors, but even this process could prove to be too trying for them in the end. Furthermore, when you gain new investors from crowdfunding, you are required legally to provide some level of ongoing disclosure to them about your company's progress, despite the fact that such a requirement is atypical for most private rounds of financing.

Herding Cats

It is often said that managing your angel investors is about as easy as herding cats; it is a statement that has persisted because it's usually true. It can be tough to deal with a large number of angels. They have egos and some may be easily distracted. As a result, I recommend that you try to limit the number of angels your company signs on to no more than five. Any more than that and you may find it tough to put together a round of funding.

Free Equity

Wait a minute, free equity? It sounds crazy, huh? Why would an entrepreneur issue shares to someone who does not pay anything for them in return? This scenario actually happens quite often when an entrepreneur brings on advisors and pays them in company shares in exchange for their expertise. Advisors can certainly be incredibly valuable, as was the case with Sean Parker, who advised Zuckerberg during Facebook's initial round of funding. Without a doubt, Parker deserved the equity he received (which, by the way, has made Parker a billionaire). However, an entrepreneur needs to be careful. There are many advisors out there who make outlandish claims about their abilities and may even lie about their backgrounds, so conduct some due diligence before bringing an advisor onboard. Another option is to ask a potential advisor to join your company on a trial basis to determine whether she can really deliver before you fork over your equity.

Venture Capital Funding

Venture Capitalists as Seed Investors

Some major VCs have begun participating in seed rounds of financing, which probably seems kind of strange. If a venture capital fund has $1 billion under management, how does it have the bandwidth to invest in many smaller deals? Don't VCs have to focus on startups that need substantial rounds of financing, such as those requiring $25 million or more? Although it is true that VCs have traditionally been involved in larger investment transactions with more mature companies, some VCs have begun trying to lock in deals with ventures while they are still in their early stages of development. To this end, VCs take a "shotgun" approach to the funding process, which means investing in as many deals as possible without doing much if any research.

Obtaining early-stage venture capital funding can be an attractive proposition for many entrepreneurs. First of all, when a VC invests in a venture early on in its development, the company's valuation tends to be higher, because the VC typically is investing only a small amount of capital and, as such, does not spend an enormous amount of time negotiating valuation figures. And, of course, when VCs are involved in early rounds of financing, a startup can potentially receive upward of $1 million in its seed round alone.

Despite these perks, receiving venture capital funding early on during your company's development could be a bad move. Why? Because unless your startup starts showing breakout momentum, your VC will probably have little or no time to devote to your venture. Furthermore, collecting early-stage venture capital funding could potentially make it more difficult for your company to raise investments during the Series A round of financing (which I discuss in the next section). How so? If your company's original VC passes on the opportunity to infuse follow-up funding into your venture during a Series A round of financing, other firms could read your VC's disinclination to invest as a sign of its lack of confidence in your venture. It's even worse if your original VC is a tier 1 firm and it provided your company with a decent amount of seed funding, such as $500,000 or more. True, maybe your VC is passing on the opportunity to invest in your company via Series A financing because it has already made major financial commitments to other companies, but prospective Series A investors won't necessarily know the true motivation behind your VC's decision to pass.

Venture Rounds

Generally speaking, founders seek out venture rounds of financing to evolve their product and to start building their company's infrastructure, which entails hiring engineers and perhaps business development people. As discussed briefly in the previous section, the first round of venture financing a founder pursues is referred to as a *Series A round*.

The total amount of financing a startup raises during a Series A round can range from $1 million to $25 million or more, but the typical amount is around $5 million to $10 million. To raise so much capital, fledgling companies generally select one lead VC whose purpose is to facilitate the financing process and bring other VCs into the round to distribute the overall risk of the investment among several parties. Keep in mind, however, superangels may also be involved in a company's Series A financing efforts. In Facebook's case, for example, Accel Partners was the only VC involved in the company's $12 million Series A round of financing in May 2005. Angel investors Marc Pincus and Reid Hoffman also participated in the round.

The Series A funding round typically lasts for a year or so. If it looks like the company will achieve longer term profitability at the conclusion of this financing process, then the company will launch a Series B round of financing to provide fuel for its growth. At this point in time, the company will probably also start exploring expansion into global markets and may bring on even more professional management to help take the venture to the next level. In some cases, the company may even acquire other ventures to help bolster its growth.

During a Series B round, a company may raise $50 million or more in financing from investors who, again, are usually VCs but may also include strategic investors. (Facebook, for example, raised $27 million from investors [including Greylock Partners, Meritech Capital Partners, and The Founders Fund] during its Series B round of financing in April 2006.) Then, when a company reaches the Series C level of financing, its investments often trickle in from several large investors over the course of several months. Typically, a startup continues raising funds in this manner via subsequent venture rounds until it is ready to go public. Or, if an IPO is not a viable option—perhaps because the market opportunity proves to be less than expected—a company may instead look to sell the company to a larger operator. This latter option, however, is not as attractive, because the returns on a company sale are generally less than they are on an IPO.

IPO Funding

When a company is ready to issue shares to the public, it undergoes a process known as an *initial public offering*, or *IPO*, and its shares are made available to the trading public via a major stock exchange, such as the NYSE or NASDAQ. Many tech companies raise upward of $100 million to $200 million during their IPOs. Facebook raised a whopping $16 billion! We look at IPOs in more detail in Chapter 14.

Types of Stock

The total number of shares available for a company to issue is referred to as *authorized stock* whereas the total number of shares that a company has already issued is referred to as *outstanding stock*. Now, let's say that company XYZ has authorized the issuance of 10 million shares of its stock, and of those 10 million shares, 1 million have already been issued. In this case, if you own 100,000 shares of XYZ, then you own a 10% stake in the company. As XYZ cycles through the various rounds of funding that a company undergoes in its development, it issues more and more of its authorized stock to early-stage investors in return for infusions of capital, which usually means that your 10% ownership stake in the company likely becomes diluted over time.

A company will issue different types of stock to different types of investors, depending on the stage of funding it's in. Common stock, for example, which represents a form of equity ownership in a company, is issued to founders, early-stage employees, and seed investors. It is also distributed, when applicable, to the startup accelerator that helped to launch the company. Angels and VCs, on the other hand, are interested in a different type of security: preferred stock. Like common stock, preferred stock bestows upon its holder equity ownership in a company, but it also confers an assortment of additional special rights, which are spelled out in the term sheet and shareholder agreements and can include liquidation preferences, veto rights, and board seats. We take a look at some additional preferred stock deal terms in chapter 6.

To continue our current discussion, however, an angel round of financing predicated on preferred stock can be time intensive (taking 2 to 4 weeks to finalize) and expensive (given that the legal costs of this process can easily soar to more than $25,000). In other words, for what amounts to a small infusion of capital——say, $500,000—preferred stock can create some big problems. To avoid the delays and expense of issuing preferred stock during the angel round of financing, founders often distribute convertible notes instead, which essentially are loans with fixed interest rates (such as 5% to 10%) that mature within 1 to 2 years of issuance. As an added bonus, interest payments are not due on accrual. Rather, any interest that accrues prior to maturity is added to the notes and can be paid off when the notes mature or are converted into equity.

Much easier to structure than preferred stock, and with legal costs that top out at maybe a few thousand dollars, convertible notes are an attractive alternative to preferred stock for founders for yet another reason: Their value is not tied to the company's overall value. As a result, convertible notes allow founders to avoid a potentially contentious conversation about company valuation with their angel investors. Might as well "kick the can down the road," right? Actually, it is rather smart for an early-stage company to put off valuation discussions because it is difficult to determine the fair value of a venture that has not yet had the time to prove its worth.

When a company is ready for a Series A round of financing, its valuation should be much easier for the founders and angels to agree on. As soon as they come to a consensus on the value of the company, the angel investors will convert their notes into preferred stock. However, convertible note holders want to receive special treatment during the Series A round in exchange for their willingness to make an initial investment in the company. You can reward your convertible note holders in one of two ways. The first approach is to put a cap on the premoney valuation of your company to ensure that note holders are cited a valuation that is no higher than a fixed amount. For example, suppose Jane invests $500,000 in XYZ. In 5 months, XYZ is funded at a premoney valuation of $20 million, but because her convertible note has a valuation cap of $5 million, Jane is cited this price when she purchases preferred stock during the company's Series A round. The second approach you can take is to give your note holder a discount, typically anywhere from 20% to 30%, on the share price of preferred stock that is issued during your Series A round.

Although it may seem unfair that you're expected to offer certain perks to early-stage investors during your company's Series A round of financing, in the long run it makes sense to keep your investors happy. After all, without a cap in place, your early-stage investors actually hope that the Series A valuation of your company is low! If they're hoping for a low valuation, what would be their incentive to help out the venture? Furthermore, because a discount or a valuation cap offered during Series A financing functions as the upside to your investors' early-stage investment, you should be able to avoid negotiating and issuing warrants, a process that can add substantially to your company's legal costs.

However, as with any financial structure, there are inherent risks involved when issuing convertible notes. After all, what if your venture doesn't get around to seeking a Series A round of financing before the note comes due?

Because the note is a debt, the holders may be able to take control of your company's assets. If you find yourself in this unfortunate situation, try to renegotiate the loan terms with your holders and find out whether they are willing to extend the notes' payment date to give your company more time to seek Series A financing.

Seed Series

During the past couple years, more and more angel investors have begun using a series seed approach to the angel round of funding, wherein they streamline the process—and expense—of issuing preferred stock by using a standardized set of financing documents rather than situation-specific legal paperwork. Be wary of this approach. Because of their fill-in-the-blank nature, series seed documents can cause you to rush the negotiation of key terms, like board seats, liquidation preferences, and so on, which is probably not the best idea in the long run. A better approach, as mentioned earlier, is issuing convertible notes.

Securities Laws

The federal government has extensive laws in place regarding the issuance of securities. If a company violates any one of these numerous laws, the federal government may require it to rescind its financing. In rare cases, the government may even impose fines and/or possibly jail sentences on the violator. Unfortunately, it is a common myth among entrepreneurs that only large companies are subject to securities laws. In reality, securities laws must be followed by *any* company that issues stock. Again, make sure that you hire competent legal counsel to guide you through the many legal complexities that arise when starting a new venture.

Know When to Raise Funds

So, when should you start the fund-raising process? Start now. In a way, a founder should *always* be fund-raising. After all, you simply do not know who you will run into, and it's surprisingly common for a casual conversation to end with someone writing a check toward your new venture. Even if you do not need the money, you should still be fund-raising constantly. Having lots of money in the bank makes it easier to avoid getting squeezed financially during those inevitable stretches of time when your company's funding dries up. Plus, you never know when the entire funding market will freeze up, as it did from 2001 to 2002 and from 2008 to 2009. During these periods, it was almost impossible for tech startups to raise sufficient capital, at least on reasonable terms. It should come as no surprise that angel investors and even professional VCs can get spooked easily, especially if the economy is in a downturn.

On a related note, never let your venture get to the point where you only have the cash to fund it for 6 more months. VCs can smell desperation and will string you along, demanding even more draconian terms in return for cash infusions. Worse yet, you may just run out of money altogether and have to close down your company's operations. Last, keep in mind that the funding process is seasonal by nature. There are two times of the year when it is almost impossible to close a funding deal: August and December. Investors are often on vacation during these months and will probably not respond to a pitch unless the deal is hot.

As described in this chapter, the funding process has many moving parts and involves many different types of investors, stages of financing, and investment structures. It can certainly get unnerving, but this is how startups have secured financing for decades. Deviating from the process is most likely a big mistake. In the next chapter, we take a look at another crucial piece of the startup puzzle, one that goes hand in hand with raising capital: the pitch. With thousands of entrepreneurs looking for capital, you need to stand out from the crowd. I'll show you how.

The Pitch

And one more thing.

—Steve Jobs

More than anything else, Mark Zuckerberg liked coding breakout apps. But as CEO of Facebook, he was forced to become intimately involved in the business side of the company, which meant he had to spend huge chunks of his time pitching—to investors, potential customers, and partners, as well as new recruits. Zuckerberg does not have the charisma of someone like Steve Jobs; he is naturally shy and a man of few words, and these qualities initially were liabilities when he attempted to pitch his company to key stakeholders. But he did not allow his natural inclinations to prevent him from getting better at pitching. In fact, Zuckerberg, recognizing his need to improve, dedicated countless hours to working on his speaking skills, and he even sought the help of speech coaches. True, he still is not as compelling a speaker as Steve Jobs was (who is!) and can seem awkward when he is giving company presentations. But when you compare Zuckerberg's early (and, it must be said, painful) interviews with the media to those he gives today, you can see how far his speaking abilities have come.

In this chapter, you will learn how to effectively pitch your deal to investors—a skill that involves more than just sounding great and convincing. You will read about the nuts and bolts of putting together key pitch documents, like your company's executive summary and slide presentation (also known as your *pitch deck* or *deck*). And you will discover how to plan your company's funding process so as to avoid common problems and errors that can kill your chances of getting a "Yes" from an investor. Let's get started.

Elevator Pitch

Even if you don't know anything else about presenting, you probably know that an *elevator pitch* is named as such because it should take you no longer than a minute or so—the length of an elevator ride—to give this quick description of your venture to a potential client or investor. Practice your elevator pitch as much as possible, until it becomes second nature. The more comfortable you are with your elevator pitch, the more likely that you can maximize each and every opportunity you get to speak with potential investors, no matter whether you meet at an event or, yes, in an elevator!

Legendary entrepreneur and angel investor Peter Thiel has a great way of expressing how an elevator pitch should be structured: Problem + Solution = Money. Thiel cites SpaceX's elevator pitch, which conforms to this model, as an example worth following: "Launch costs haven't come down in decades. We slash them by 90%. The market is worth $10 billion." The pitch is incredibly simple, but it has proven to be equally compelling. After all, SpaceX has raised hundreds of millions of dollars from some of the world's best investors, including Thiel.

The Deck

As mentioned previously, when pitching to potential investors, you are expected to provide them with a set of slides, also known as a deck, that illustrates and augments your formal verbal presentation. Because your deck will be a key focus for investors, plan on spending quite a bit of time putting the deck together. But before you jump into the deck creation process just yet, be sure to avoid the following deck mistakes commonly made by entrepreneurs:

- *Clutter:* Keep the text in your deck to an absolute minimum. Practice giving your pitch to your co-founders and employees and ask them to help you identify text-heavy slides that would benefit from pruning. VCs don't have time to review a deck that is filled with prose, so wherever possible, try to use visuals and pictures to make your points.

- *Don't assume:* Although it is generally true that VCs are smart people, you should never assume that they understand everything about your business. If a specific aspect of your business is too specialized or complex for the average businessperson to grasp, then it is a good idea to spell out that component for your VCs as well. The last thing you want is for your VCs to lose interest or patience in your venture simply because they don't understand one of its features.

- *Hollywood:* Over the past few years, many entrepreneurs have begun using Hollywood-style pitch techniques, wherein they say something like, "Our app is like Facebook . . . but for businesses." Although this approach can be somewhat helpful in explaining your product to investors, it comes off as unoriginal.

- *PDFs:* Avoid presenting your company's financials on PDFs, which are static files that cannot be modified. You should instead use Excel files, because investors will want to play around with your financial model and check its underlying assumptions.

- *The exit:* When you are ready to wrap up your presentation and explain your exit strategy, avoid saying something like, "We plan to sell our company for $100 million in 2 years." Contrary to what you might expect, VCs aren't necessarily interested in a quick cash-out; they realize that five to ten years will most likely pass before a viable exit option presents itself. So instead of telling your VCs what you think they want to hear, show them that you are committed to the venture for the long haul. Otherwise, they may begin to fear that you won't stick around to see your venture through to fruition.

Now that we've covered what you shouldn't do with regard to deck writing, what are some common features of winning decks? First, good decks are short, containing no more than 12 slides. (By way of comparison, Facebook's original deck was only six slides long!) But if your current deck is 25 slides long and you think you can shorten it simply by jamming content drawn from 5 of your slides onto 1 using a miniscule font, think again. Any text that appears in your deck should be typed in a font that is at least 30 points in size. Your deck should also focus heavily on your company's *proof points*, or the major, tangible signs that suggest your business has a lot of potential. Facebook's deck, for example, showed that the company had achieved massive growth in users, but it also demonstrated that the company had been able to foster a high level of engagement on the site, given that about 65% of users were returning to Facebook on a daily basis. And you better believe that this stat grabbed the instant attention of Facebook's VCs!

Your presentation should last about 30 to 45 minutes, but don't be alarmed if you are cut off with questions before you've had the chance to present all of your slides. Questions are an indicator that the VCs in the room are interested in your company and are already starting to think about its potential and possibilities, so try to refrain from interrupting the natural flow of questions and answers to return to your slides. There's nothing like an energy-charged brainstorming session to increase your potential investors' enthusiasm in your company.

As for what types of slides you should include in your deck, the following are a few to consider.

Mission

To get your deck off to a powerful start and immediately grab the attention of your investors, think about launching the deck with a slide that outlines your company's mission and reveals how your product will help change the world. You may want to supplement the text description of your mission with a visual. This could be a graphic of your product or something that shows the growth rate, such as an upward-sloping chart.

Product

If your deck focuses too much on features and delves too deeply into the technology that underpins your product, you run the risk of losing your audience's attention. Investors don't care what type of server you use to host your product; instead, they want to know what kinds of problems your product will solve. Will it help users cut their costs? Increase their revenues? Gain access to better information? Facebook, for example, makes it possible for users to instantaneously and continuously connect with their friends and colleagues, no matter how geographically separated they may be. As most Facebook users would agree, the site sure beats old-world communication solutions, which tend to be slow and difficult to maintain.

When describing your product in your deck, you should also answer the following two questions:

Question #1: Why is your approach superior to others that are currently in use or development?

Answer #1: It helps if you are focused on solving just a couple of people's most pressing problems. Facebook, for example, had the single-minded goal of making it extremely easy for users to connect with their friends and share information and photos. As a result, Zuckerberg launched only a handful of major features—like the News Feed and Photos—every year or so. He also refrained from cluttering the site with advertisements, which would have detracted from the user experience. This approach was in stark contrast to

Facebook's competitors, such as MySpace, which were scattered web sites that often confused users and annoyed them with offers and even spam.

Question #2: What prevents your competitors from copying your product and killing it?

Answer #2: You need to be able to show potential investors that you have unfair advantages over your competition. Facebook had a top-notch technology infrastructure, which allowed users to rapidly download pages, photos, and videos. Meanwhile, Facebook's competitors—MySpace and Friendster—had fairly weak technology foundations that detracted from the user experience, and as a result, these sites eventually faded away. Keep in mind that most companies' unfair advantages are behind the scenes, hidden from users' view. What Zuckerberg realized is that users don't care *how* the technology works; they just want it to work, and they want it to work quickly—which explains why Facebook spent so much time recruiting top-notch software engineers.

Spend a lot of time thinking about these two questions. VCs want to understand your thinking process and strategic ability—and with good reason! After all, they are about to shell out millions of dollars to fund your dream, so it's reasonable that they want to have a firm grasp on what sets your venture apart from the thousands of others out there.

The Opportunity

As a general rule, VCs will not fund a product unless it has at least a $1 billion target market, so if your end product is only meant to fit the needs of a smaller market, you probably won't get much interest from VCs. This is not to say, however, that you should abandon your work on a product that is *initially* intended for a niche audience and start the product development process all over again, this time with an emphasis on creating a product that is targeted to everyone and their mother. Although it may seem counterintuitive, it actually is a smart idea to focus on a small part of the market when you are first launching your product. Doing so allows you to test the product and get user feedback prior to a larger product rollout. What's more, due to its size, your test market is likely underserved, and so your product may gain much more traction than it would if you released it to your eventual intended user base all at once.

Think about how Facebook handled its product rollout. Initially started at Harvard, Facebook caught on quickly in its first small target market. Word about a new online social network spread organically from college to college, and eventually students from colleges and universities around the country began lobbying the site for access. In response, Facebook started to slowly roll out the site to more and more schools, continuously testing and refining the concept with each new school that was added to the network.

Interestingly enough, if Facebook had limited itself to the college market, the company probably would not have been able to grab the attention of potential VCs. But even though it was launched into a small market, Facebook was never in danger of limiting its potential for growth. Zuckerberg was well aware of the widespread appeal of his idea. He saw the college market as a stepping stone in Facebook's larger journey to becoming the social network for the globe. In choosing to start small, Zuckerberg made a strategic decision that allowed him to demonstrate to VCs how his service worked in smaller markets and ensure that his vision for the site was as easy to understand as possible.

When it comes to developing a slide about your company's market opportunity, a common approach many entrepreneurs take is to detail their total addressable market (TAM), which consists of the likely purchasers of your product or service. One company whose TAM surprised just about everyone is Zappos. At first, when Zappos was getting off the ground, it seemed outlandish that people would buy shoes online. Isn't it essential to try them on before buying them? But Tony Hsieh, an initial investor in and now the current CEO of Zappos, realized the market opportunity of the online retail giant thanks to an analogy that its founder, Nick Swinmurn, pointed out in his pitch to Hsieh's investment firm, Venture Frogs. In 1999, the US shoe industry amounted to about \$40 billion, and about \$2 billion—or 5%—of this revenue came from mail-order purchases. Swinmurn (rightly) surmised that this sales figure would rise if shoes were available for purchase online, especially because the buying experience would be interactive. Hsieh thought that Swinmurn's reasoning made a lot of sense and invested in Zappos, which, as most of us would agree, was a wise decision.

Team

Unless you have a good track record of starting successful companies, you need to assemble a reliable, committed, full-time, and preferably experienced team prior to launching your venture. Otherwise, potential VCs may view your company with trepidation and be reluctant to pull the trigger on funding. We hope you have already filled some of the key spots on your team and identified, say, your lead technology person, or someone who has deep domain experience. But don't feel as though you have to sign on partners purely for the sake of impressing potential VCs with a huge team roster. Your core team need only consist of three or four people, as long as you can offer VCs some tangible evidence that these are the people who will take your company to great heights.

On your team slide, you should include simple bios for each member of your company. Figure 5-1 gives an example.

Jane Smith, Chief Technology Officer	Engineering team for Facebook Payments (security) Engineer at Google's Android (payment gateways)

Figure 5-1. Example of showing your team member on a slide

Focus on each team member's relevant experience, and, yes, be concise. When discussing your team in your pitch deck, you should also cover these additional factors:

- What's your approach to compensation?

- What additional talent are you planning to recruit?

- How do you plan to recruit them?

Business Model

Be sure to include a slide or two in your deck that shows potential VCs how your venture will make money. After all, the main reason you're pitching to them in the first place is because you want them to fund your company in return for a slice of its equity. If you haven't developed at least an initial strategy to monetize your business and earn your VCs a return on their investment, well, then, what incentive do they have to invest? Sure, it's tough to know how your product will evolve and what types of customers you'll have, so your company's initial business model may very well be off the mark. Facebook's original business model, for example, was local advertising! But crafting a well-thought-out business model demonstrates to VCs that your company is a worthwhile investment.

Your business model need not be complicated. Airbnb's pitch deck included a straightforward slide that detailed the company's business model. It said, simply, "We take a 10% commission on each transaction." The slide then indicated that, based on its sales history, the company received roughly $20 per transaction. This sent a compelling message to Airbnb's VCs, because they could immediately do the mental math and realize that a few million transactions would ensure that the company becomes a breakout success.

Turn to Chapter 9 for more details on the various approaches your company can take to generating revenue.

Go-to-Market Strategy

Often, new ventures pay little attention to their go-to-market strategy in their pitch deck, despite the fact that it is absolutely critical to demonstrate that they have rigorously analyzed and mapped out their product's distribution channels. After all, few products sell themselves or somehow go viral.

VCs want to see that a startup has some creative, grassroots marketing strategies. If you're looking for examples of startups with unconventional marketing tactics, look no further than Mint's Aaron Patzer. Before Patzer launched his app, he started a financial blog that catered to his app's eventual target demographic—twentysomethings—and covered topics like credit cards, school loans, and career tips. As it turned out, Patzer's blog helped so much with his branding efforts and collected so many e-mail addresses—by the time Mint was ready to be launched, he had amassed more than 20,000 members—that he was able to catch the attention of VCs, who felt better about funding the company.

Chapter 7 looks at various approaches to distribution in much more detail. For now, remember that no matter what go-to-market strategy (or strategies!) fit your product best, you should make sure your deck covers this key topic.

Competition

Name your company's top rivals in your deck, and explain how your product and company are different from the competition. Never say, "We have no competition," a phrase that is almost always untrue and has the unique ability to make potential VCs cringe.

Sometimes your competition may not even be a company. Instead, you could be competing against an old and established way that customers do something. Just look at the highly popular music streaming service Spotify, whose founder and CEO, Daniel Ek, says his competition is piracy. To ensure his company's success, Ek built a service with an easy-to-use, fast interface that makes music sharing among friends not just possible but a cinch. Thanks to Spotify, music piracy doesn't seem all that attractive any more.

Financial Forecast

Early-stage VCs expect you to divulge your company's monthly revenue and expense forecast for its first year of operations in your pitch deck. Then, after your company has celebrated its one-year anniversary, you're expected to revise these figures and break out your forecasts on an annualized—rather than monthly—basis for the next two years your company is in business. Insert all this information into a spreadsheet, and don't forget to include some basic financial modeling, such as a formula that shows how many customers you will attract for a given amount of expenditures on sales and marketing, as well as an estimate of the average revenue your company will take in per customer. Once you compile these financial details, you will have created a decent revenue forecast.

Although educated guesses suffice on the revenue side of the financial forecast equation, be sure to provide your VCs with a detailed analysis of your company's expected expenses, the majority of which will most likely result from hiring new employees. But keep in mind that even though you will delve deeply into the details when considering your company's likely expenses, you still will almost certainly underestimate the costs of running your business. Trust me on this one: for any given period of operations, take the total amount of your expected costs and multiply that figure by 1.5. The result of this calculation is a much more realistic estimate of your company's overall costs for that period.

When you have finished your spreadsheet, summarize the key points of your financial forecast on a slide in your pitch deck. Check out the sample financial forecast slide pictured in Table 5-1 (the numbers are in thousands).

Table 5-1. Sample of a company's financial projections

	2013	2014	2015
Users	250	1,300	6,250
Revenues	$1,500	$9,333	$62,500
Sales and Marketing	$5,000	$20,000	$50,000
General and Administrative	$500	$1,000	$4,000
Research and Development	$1,000	$4,000	$8,000
Cash Flow	($5,000)	($15,667)	$500
Revenues per User	$6	$7	$10
Marketing costs per User	$20	$15	$8

Do not insert any fancy financial metrics, like your company's discounted cash flow or your internal rate of return, into your financial forecast spreadsheet. Such details are overkill and provide potential VCs with little information about the opportunity your venture presents. Be an entrepreneur—not an MBA!

Financing

Be sure to review your company's financing history in your pitch deck, including the specific amount of money you want to raise during the round of funding in which you are currently immersed. And do not suggest that you are open to receiving a range of funding, because VCs may take this as a reason to fund your venture at the low end of your specified range.

Conclusion

When you are ready to wrap up your pitch deck, you need a final slide that gives your VCs an overview of the most important takeaways from your presentation and is sure to leave a long-lasting impression. Think about reemphasizing your company's mission and revisiting the ways in which your product will help to change the world. This way, you begin your presentation powerfully and conclude it just as powerfully.

Seeing Is Believing

A pitch deck is an important component of your presentation to potential VCs, but it can only take you so far. If you truly want to grab the attention of investors, show up at your pitch meetings with a prototype of your product. It does not have to be a finished product; it can be a crude version of what's to come. As long as potential investors can toy around with your prototype (which they love to do, by the way!), they can better visualize the opportunity your company and product represent—and they may come up with some ideas that prove invaluable to your company's and product's future development.

A working prototype certainly was advantageous to Facebook's funding efforts. After all, the site was already up and running—and gaining hordes of new users every day—by the time Zuckerberg began pitching to VCs. To be sure, Facebook's potential investors still had many questions and concerns about the site, but it was hard to argue about the fact that the company was gaining traction with its users on a daily basis.

In some instances, in lieu of presenting a deck at its pitch meetings, a company simply chooses to demo its product for potential investors. Instagram went this route when its product was still a minimum viable product (MVP)—which, in tech lingo, means the product was in its raw stages and focused on just a few core functions. The concept of what qualifies as an MVP is fuzzy, though. Some entrepreneurs believe that a handful of screenshots or an extremely crude prototype can be considered an MVP; but when it comes to securing funding, these looser definitions are probably too minimal. This is not to say that you must spend months developing a prototype of your product. Countless great products, from Facebook to GroupMe, have had short development cycles and were created in a minimal amount of time. But in the end, your prototype should be robust enough to demonstrate to potential investors that your product is a source of value for users.

Executive Summary and Business Plan

Before you walk into a pitch meeting with potential VCs, you should draft a concise executive summary whose purpose it is to express the core elements of your business by transforming your deck into paragraph form. Try to limit your executive summary to one page, which should be enough space for you to give investors a good idea of what your business is all about. If you must go over that in length, be sure to cap the document at no more than three pages.

Some general rules to follow when writing your executive summary are as follows:

- Avoid buzzwords, which annoy VCs and may give the impression that your business is a farce.

- Write in clear sentences. It's okay for your executive summary to be conversational in nature, but don't fill the document with jokes and witticisms. The purpose of an executive summary is not to draw a laugh; it's to get to the point.

- Keep the graphics to a minimum. It may be a good idea to include a screenshot of your product and a chart of your company's progress, but don't forget that the document should be heavier on text and lighter on images.

What about a formal business plan? Forget about it; formal business plans are a waste of time—so much so that, nowadays, VCs do not expect you to provide one. But it is a good idea to craft an operating plan, whose purpose it is to act as a guide to your business's objectives for the next year and provide a detailed, month-by-month description of stated goals. An operating plan is an extremely useful tool for keeping a venture on track and measuring the progress it makes. If things begin to slip and your company fails to meet its monthly goals, an operating plan can help put you back on course.

An operating plan may include the following components:

- *Product specification:* Generally a few pages in length, your product specification should describe the main objectives of your product. Limit your description to include three or four features.

- *Product map:* Anticipate how your users will navigate your product, and describe that process in your product map.

- *Product copy:* The messaging of your product is vital, so don't forget to consider the copy you use to describe your web site or mobile app. If your value proposition is instantly clear to users when they check out your product, they are more likely to adopt it.

- *Hiring plan:* List the open positions for which you still need to hire. Include the ideal skill sets of and compensation levels for each of these future employees. Also define each future recruit's goals.

You can include your operating plan in the due-diligence materials you gather for your VCs. Although drafting an operating plan may feel like a lot of work at first, the forethought you put into this document is likely to provide comfort to VCs and increase their willingness to invest. After all, a well-thought-out operating plan shows that you have a disciplined approach to growing your company.

Rookie Mistakes When Making the Pitch

It's inevitable that you'll make lots of mistakes along your entrepreneurial journey, and the good news is that these slip-ups more often than not serve as great learning experiences. But some mistakes can be easily avoided. Here are the most common mistakes new entrepreneurs make when raising capital:

- *Requesting a signature on a nondisclosure agreement (NDA):* Regardless of how great or groundbreaking your product is, a reputable investor will not sign an NDA because doing so could prevent them from looking at more deals. It may even lead to lawsuits.

- *Sending unsolicited e-mail to an investor:* If you are targeting top investors, sending them unsolicited e-mails is a big waste of time. These types of e-mails are almost in line with those that everyone seems to get from Nigeria, asking the recipient to pony up $10,000 cash in return for a $10 million reward! The best way to connect with a qualified investor is through a referral or an introduction—not an unsolicited e-mail.

- *Pitching to the wrong investor:* Many angels and VCs focus on specific tech categories, investment levels, geographies, and so on. Before making your pitch, do some research on the investor to ensure that your business interests and theirs are aligned.

- *Asking for a referral:* If an investor tells you, "No," then take it at face value and, more important, do not ask for a referral for other investors. Doing so creates an uncomfortable situation. Besides, do you really think the VC will make an enthusiastic introduction for you?

- *Don't hit your head against the wall:* If you aren't getting much interest from your pitch, then you need to revaluate the situation. What's the problem? What parts of your pitch are being met with the most skepticism? Figure out what's broken, and fix it. If you don't, you'll probably remain on the proverbial treadmill.

Presentation Skills

Without a doubt, giving your pitch can be a nerve-wracking experience. It's not easy to anticipate the questions that potential investors may have, and it's also tough to engage their interest. Are they zoning out and thinking about other transactions? Or are they engrossed in your presentation and brainstorming new applications for your product?

Fortunately, there are a few tricks you can deploy when giving your pitch that might help improve your odds:

- *Timing:* Try to schedule your meetings with potential investors in the morning. The VCs will be more energized and less frazzled, which means they should be able to focus on your deal more. By the afternoon, however, they may want to bolt from the office.

- *Funny:* Don't be overly serious in your presentation, because this can be a big turn-off for investors. Instead, try to be loose and conversational. It's also a big help if you can provide some humor—but don't go overboard. One joke is fine.

- *RetailRoadshow.com:* This web site hosts videotaped pre-sentations given by executives of companies that are up for IPOs. No doubt, the CEOs featured in the videos are pros at raising capital, and as a result, it may prove helpful to study their presentations. You can also get slide ideas from their decks.

Practice Meetings and Plan of Attack

It's a good idea to test your pitch—but not on VCs with whom you want to make a deal. You should never throw away a meeting on a must-have investor just for the sake of refining your presentation. Instead, before you begin scheduling meetings with VCs to whom you want to make a real pitch, you should start by pitching friendlies, who may include your advisors, trusted friends, and investors you are not particularly interested in working with.

The more you pitch, the better off you'll be. You should be able to do it almost reflexively while making certain your pitch is natural and smooth—which shouldn't be a problem if you believe in your company's mission. When getting feedback on your performance, tell your listeners not to hold back with their criticism and comments. Sure, it can be brutal and uncomfortable to be informed of your shortcomings, but if you want to become a pro at raising capital, you need to know your weaknesses.

Once you feel comfortable giving your pitch, put together a fundraising plan that outlines the steps you plan to take—as well as the timeframe in which you'll take them—to finance your company. Keep in mind that raising capital can be a time sink—a Series A round of financing alone can take anywhere from one to three months to complete—and your pitch is just the start of the fundraising process. You also need to allot sufficient time to engage in negotiations, perform due diligence, and finalize the transaction.

But don't give yourself too much time to complete your fundraising plan. Why? Because it is very easy to lose your focus on managing your company during the fundraising process. It makes sense, right? The more time you spend pitching VCs, negotiating terms, and signing contracts, the less time you have to commit to the essential day-to-day operations of your company. What's more, VCs have a good sense of when a company is deteriorating, and they usually are not afraid to take advantage of the situation.

A shortened fundraising schedule is also important because of the tight-knit nature of the VC community. When VCs see a deal they are interested in, they tell their friends at other firms about it, which helps build buzz for the company in question. Then, if word spreads that the company is approaching potential deals with a sense of speed and urgency, investors may jump on board simply because they don't want to miss the train before it leaves the station. On the other hand, if the buzzed-about company spaces out its meetings and drags its feet on drafting term sheets for investors, the initial buzz and enthusiasm surrounding the company may subside, diminishing the company's investment prospects in the process.

So, how do you avoid creating a time-intensive fundraising plan? Easy: condense the time period you have designated for fundraising. Draw up a list of VCs you want to pitch to, and schedule your meetings with them during a short time period. The latter shouldn't be too difficult to achieve, because many VCs in Silicon Valley (at least the ones that matter) are concentrated along Sand Hill Road. As much as possible, talk to lead investors, which are firms that manage the investment process for your company. If you have several lead investors at the table, you may be able to create a bidding frenzy, which will lead to a higher valuation for your company—not to mention a shortened fundraising period!

Finding the Right VCs

When it comes to finding the right VCs for your company, avoid using a "spray and pray" approach. Instead, target the VCs who are best suited for getting your company to its next level of growth. How do you do that? Go beyond the brand name of the firm and look at the other companies they've invested in, the stage of development they prefer a company to be in before making an investment, and what their investment successes have been. In other words, you should do a background check on a VC firm and its partners before requesting a meeting with them. You can start by doing a Google search on the firm in question and then asking your shared contacts about their experiences with the firm. Does the investor have a background in your company's space? Can they bring strong contacts to the table? What about good advice? Or are they known to be a troublemaker? If the answers to these questions don't meet your standards, don't be afraid to walk away from the firm. It's never easy to say "No" to someone who's willing to write you a check, but in some cases, doing so may be the best decision.

Once you have compiled a short list of preferred investors, ask your mutual contacts for an introduction. It may also be worthwhile to have a two-minute phone call with each of your potential investors before setting up a formal pitch meeting with them. On the call, give the VC your elevator pitch and see if they have any interest in your company. If the investor's enthusiasm is lacking, well, that's one less needless presentation you have to make.

Data Room

Data rooms are secure online portals with limited controlled access that allow investors to log in and view your investor materials, including your deck, executive summary, and due-diligence information. Although using a data room to store your company's documentation may at first seem unnecessary, investors appreciate being able to access all of your company's investor materials on one central hub. What's more, constant e-mailing back and forth of documents can slow the investment process—or result in errors.

If you're looking for a secure data room for your company, you might consider using CapLinked, which caters to early-stage companies, is easy to use, and can be integrated with outside resources, such as LinkedIn. Perhaps the most important feature of CapLinked, though, is its ability to let you know that an investor has looked at your company's materials. If an investor has indeed been reviewing your company on the site, you may notice, based on the specific documents they downloaded, that they seem to be interested in your company's business model and product. This information can be extremely helpful to you when reaching out to the investor in question.

Be Wary of the Fake VC

It may be difficult to believe, but some VCs don't have any money to invest. Consider that a typical VC fund progresses through several key stages in its lifespan, one of which occurs during the fund's second to third year, when its partners start to raise capital for the firm's next fund. If the returns on the prior fund have been lackluster, investors may not have any interest in joining the next fund—which means the fund won't have any money to invest. So, if you notice that a VC firm hasn't made an investment in a year or so, steer clear. This type of inactivity is almost always a sure sign that the firm has run out of investable capital.

On a related note, you should also be wary if you discover that one of the top partners at a firm has stepped down or switched employers. Why? Because, often, investors and VC firms sign agreements stipulating that the fund's investing activity will be halted if one of the firm's main partners pulls out. A clause of this nature is perfectly reasonable; after all, investors decide which funds to invest in based on the skills and reputations of those funds' main partners. Why, then, would they leave their money in a fund that is managed by someone they don't trust?

Don't Get Too Excited

I often hear entrepreneurs say something like: "I talked to this VC the other day, and he was really excited about my company." Not to be rude, but so what? VCs are smart and calculating individuals, which is why they generally refrain from saying "No" to any deal. What if that company becomes the next

Facebook? Saying "No" to a company takes VCs out of the game, and they always want to make sure they are in the game—just in case.

You also must realize that there is an important pecking order in the VC world, and titles matter. If you talk to a director, a principal, an associate, or a research analyst about your company, you aren't talking to a decision-maker. People in these types of positions almost never say "No" because they are mostly keeping track of the players in the market, not making crucial decisions about which companies get what amount of funding. But if you do manage to talk to a firm's managing director or general partner, congratulations: you are talking to a decision-maker. What's more, they have little time to spare, so the fact that they are willing to meet you is a very good sign. In this case, you can get a little excited!

Thick Skin

Unless you have developed a super-hot product, expect to be rejected by VCs. Any company that is attempting to pioneer a new approach should expect its fair share of rejections. And when those inevitable rejections start trickling in, chin up: investors passed on Facebook in the belief that it was overvalued or a fad. Remember, raising money is like any others sales process. You have a target audience, and there is a hit rate. If things go well, several VCs will compete for your deal.

Let the World Know

When you close a round of funding, draft a press release that features quotes from some of the VC partners who have invested in your company; this will add credibility to your venture. You should also add an "Investor" section to your company web site that includes information about the company's funding as well as a contact name, a phone number, and an e-mail address.

Next, typically several days prior to your company's official funding announcement, reach out to some of the typical blogs in your sector and alert them to the news of your funding. Reporters generally hold off on announcing such news before the predetermined announcement date you set for them, but be aware that embargos may be broken. Sure, this may be a bummer, but at least you are getting exposure for your company.

Leverage Your Investors

Many entrepreneurs have little idea how to enlist their investors' help. In some cases, entrepreneurs may see their investors as adversaries, especially if funding negotiations were contentious. But this is a big mistake. Angels and VCs generally have a tremendous amount of entrepreneurial and business experience, so get your investors involved in your company as much as possible. If you are having trouble finding ways to make the most of your investors' skills and talents, try these strategies:

- Ask for their advice on the new iteration of your product.

- Request that they help you lure in new hires.

- Propose that they put you in touch with companies with which you are interested in forming partnerships.

- Suggest that they give you feedback on your company's new marketing campaign.

You don't have to involve every investor in every decision you make. Instead, segment them into their areas of expertise, which should help streamline the advice-gathering process—and maximize your results.

Summary

As you can see in this chapter, you need to display a tremendous amount of sales savvy when dealing with investors. In fact, being a skilled salesperson is critical if you want to achieve success as an entrepreneur, because you are, in parallel, selling not only to investors but to potential employees and customers as well. Selling yourself, your company, and your product may be a somewhat uncomfortable experience, but you don't have much choice in the matter. When in doubt, repeat to yourself: "Sales is not evil!"

In the next chapter, we look at the nitty-gritty of negotiating an offer from investors. It's an intense process, but I'll show you some ways to get your footing.

Deal Terms

My father said: You must never try to make all the money that's in a deal. Let the other fellow make some money too, because if you have a reputation for always making all the money, you won't have many deals.

—J. Paul Getty

When an angel or VC wants to make an investment, they issue a *term sheet*. This is a short document—one to four pages or so—that sets forth the amount to be invested and the valuation. There is also an array of protections that are heavily legalistic and technical. Often these are the most critical part of the document, yet investors tend to focus instead on the valuation. It can be a huge mistake.

Mark Zuckerberg agreed to his first term sheet back in 2005, which came from Peter Thiel. Mark had the help of counsel and key advisors like Sean Parker, who understood the nuances of the deal terms. Although the valuation was important, it didn't become an obsession. Consider that an important focus was for Mark to maintain control of Facebook, which would prove critical for the company's success.

All this required hefty legal fees, which were the company's responsibility. And did you know that general practice is for the company to also pay the VC's fees? It's true. But these come out of the financing.

This chapter shows many of the types of provisions you see in a term sheet and how to negotiate them. After this, you will look at how to manage the due-diligence process, which can have its own landmines. But first let's cover some time-honored approaches to smart negotiation.

Being a Dealmaker

Before getting into the negotiating process, make sure your team is on the same page. This includes not only your co-founders but also your advisors and attorneys. Decide on things like the ideal term sheet you want, deal killers, the minimum levels on key points, and terms that don't matter much.

You'll be glad you vetted these issues. Keep in mind that VCs are pros at negotiation—it's part of their job description—and are not afraid to pounce on inexperienced entrepreneurs.

Let's say one co-founder blurts out that an anti-dilution clause is important, but a few days later another co-founder mentions the opposite. The VC will smell an opportunity to kick out the clause.

Yes, it can be brutal.

Negotiating Tips

It's common for entrepreneurs to talk too much in negotiations. This may be due to nervousness, or it may be a way to create rapport.

Don't fall into this trap. You may talk too loosely about certain terms, such as inadvertently volunteering your minimum deal points on the valuation or the liquidation preference. It's almost impossible to undue such a move.

What about Zuckerberg? By his nature, he is a quiet person. He reflects much on ideas and what people say. The silent approach has also been a great negotiating technique. Despite his young age, he was able to effectively go up against some of the world's best dealmakers.

If you read the literature on negotiation—and there are many books on the topic—you'll notice myriad approaches. One is to be Mr. Nice Guy and not get too aggressive. The belief is that you'll reach a better deal if you're collaborative.

There are merits to this technique, but it has its problems. Investors want to know that an entrepreneur is tough and willing to fight hard on material points. If you roll over on major issues of the financing, you'll probably lose the confidence of your potential investors. They will wonder: Are you too wishy-washy? Will you be up to the task of getting strong terms from customers and vendors? Probably not. Consider that investors, such as Peter Thiel, have passed on investments because the entrepreneurs were not willing to get aggressive on their negotiations.

On other hand, some entrepreneurs go to the other extreme, taking a no-prisoner's approach. The premise is that a negotiation is a war, and every point must be won.

The most notable example is Steve Jobs, who was a relentless negotiator. Somehow he was able to get his way with mega companies.

But of course, Jobs was an outlier. He had an innate sense of timing and immense charisma. Chances are you don't. So if you are too hostile in your negotiations, you'll likely wind up with little to nothing to show for it. It's also important to remember that during the negotiation process, you are in the early stages of building a relationship with the VCs. They will be part of your company for years.

The best negotiating approach is to maintain a balance between collaboration and aggression. It's not easy, but it gets better with experience—and as an entrepreneur, you will have many opportunities for practice. It's key to be mindful of the balance and keep finding ways to improve.

You should also be wary if the VC uses hostile tactics. Is this approach the typical way they conduct business? Might this bode ill for a long-term relationship?

One bad sign is if the VC offers an *exploding term sheet*, which means you must agree to it within a short period of time (say, 24 to 48 hours). This high-pressure technique is a major red flag. Probably the best thing to do is walk away.

You also should not agree to a "representations and warranty" clause that makes you personally responsible for the company's results. This could be devastating to your personal finances. It also shows that the VC is overreaching and you should probably look elsewhere for an investor.

Get Some Thick Skin

If a VC gives a low-ball number on your company's valuation, it feels like an insult. You may want to lash out or tank the deal. Don't they know this company has huge potential?

This may be the case, but you need to realize that VCs are taking a big leap of faith. Most early-stage ventures fail for a host of reasons, such as timing, competition, and bad execution.

It's amazing that VCs are willing to invest in such ventures. Doesn't it seem nuts to put $5 million into a company that has only a prototype, no sales, and a young management team?

So when it comes to the valuation of your company, you need to have thick skin. Expect the low-ball offers—and don't be surprised if the valuation goes even lower as the negotiation progresses! It's all part of the not-so-glamorous journey for an entrepreneur.

A big fear of entrepreneurs is a massive dilution of their ownership stake. It could mean the difference between being mega-wealthy or moderately wealthy or merely content. But there is no way around dilution; it's part of the game. As for Zuckerberg, he had only 28.1% of Facebook's ownership when the company came public in May 2012. But it was still enough to make him one of the world's richest people.

Valuation Is an Art, Not a Science

There are several approaches to valuing a company. They include looking at comparable transactions, coming up with the market values of the assets, and evaluating a company's cash flows.

But for early-stage ventures, none of these methods work. Even if there are similar transactions, they won't have been disclosed. An early-stage company has few meaningful assets, and cash flows are years away. So throw away your Excel spreadsheets—they're useless and will muck things up.

Perhaps the only quantitative standard is that an investor generally takes a minority stake in an early-stage company, say 10% to 40%. By doing so, they make sure the entrepreneurs have enough incentive to create a breakout company.

The ownership percentage varies based on a variety of factors. One is the general funding environment. If it's robust—like the late 1990s or 2010 to 2012—then expect the ownership percentage to be 10% to 15%. But if the market is in a nuclear winter, such as during 2001 to 2003, then it could be 30% to 40%. This is assuming any investors are willing to write a check.

The other critical factor for the valuation of the company is its hotness. If you have what appears to be the next Facebook, then expect multiple term sheets, all with minimal valuation percentages (they could easily be below 10%). But for this to happen, you need to have tremendous traction in the marketplace already.

The more likely scenario is that there will be naysayers. VCs will try to get a better ownership percentage by highlighting the risks. This is why you need to constantly find ways to hit milestones and show ongoing progress. It's the only way to get a blow-out valuation.

Types of Valuations

To negotiate the valuation, you first need to understand the lingo. Keep in mind that there are two types of valuations: pre-money and post-money.

The *pre-money* is the valuation of the company before any capital is added. Suppose you start a company, and, based on your analysis, you think it's worth $5 million. This is the pre-money valuation.

Let's say an investor agrees to this amount and is willing to invest $1 million. In this case, the *post-money* valuation is $6 million, which is the pre-money valuation plus the investment amount.

As you can see, the difference between the pre- and post-money valuations is $1 million, which is significant. This is why you need to be clear with the VC about which one is being discussed. If not, you may wind up with less equity. VCs understand this and are not afraid to confuse matters to get an edge.

But there is another wrinkle—and this is mostly for Series A deals. An investor will require that a certain amount of equity be set aside for options for employees; this is called an *option pool.*

Again, make sure you and the investor are talking about the right valuation. Is it before the option pool is added or after? If it's the former, you will suffer from dilution over time as you grant options. This can be a big deal, because option pools typically range from 10% to 20% of the outstanding shares. In the case of the Series A funding of Facebook, the company and the VC agreed to share the dilution of the option pool. It was a reasonable approach.

If this is not possible, you can try to get a higher pre-money valuation. But this has its limits as well. Unless you have a red-hot startup, you may not be in a position to get aggressive about the valuation.

Finally, you need to understand that there are valuation differences for the types of securities involved in the financing. In general, common stock is valued at 10% of preferred stock, because the preferred stock has more power. Although this may seem a bit unfair, it's actually a benefit to the company. A lower valuation on the common stock makes it easier for employees and founders to buy shares, because they are much cheaper.

The 10% rule is also a way to avoid tax problems. For example, let's say the common stock is sold at 1 cent per share to the founders. Six months later, they sell shares to angels at $1 per share. In this case, the IRS will wonder if the original valuation was too low, and the founders may have to pay a huge tax bill. By having separate valuations for the common and preferred stock, you can avoid this problem.

Critical Deal Terms

Don't get deeply mired in all of a term sheet's clauses. Many are not particularly important and are a waste of time. When getting funding, you want to maintain momentum and close the deal quickly so you can begin the next phase of the company's growth.

Speed is also important because the funding environment can freeze in an instant. Take the example of PayPal. The company's CEO, Peter Thiel, rushed to close a $100 million funding in March 2000 because he thought the dot-com bubble would burst. He turned out to be prescient: the market collapsed in a few days. Without the funding, PayPal would have been out of cash in about two months.

There will inevitably be disagreement, but the most important clauses in a term sheet include the liquidation preference, the board slots, anti-dilution, pay to play, and drag-along rights. Let's look at each in more detail:

Liquidation Preference

The liquidation preference gives priority to the investor when there is a liquidity event, such as an acquisition. The most basic is a *1X preference*. This means the investor gets up to 1 times the investment back before anyone else gets any cash.

This is a reasonable provision. To understand it, here's an example. Jack raises $5 million for his startup. After a few months, he gets bored with the venture and shuts down operations. He walks away with a big chunk of the money because he owns more than a majority of the stock. It's sounds awful, but it's perfectly legal.

Because of this potential scenario, you have no choice but to accept a liquidation preference. Even Facebook had to.

The good news is that you can soften the impact. If an investor demands a 2X or 3X or even 4X preference, push back hard. It could mean you wind up with absolutely nothing even if your company turns out to be a success.

For example, suppose you get a $10 million investment, but there is a 3X liquidation preference. If you receive a $30 million buyout, all of it goes to the investors. In the end, you will have been an employee, not an entrepreneur.

A VC may try to extract even more with something called a *participation*, which gives them part of the upside as well. Let's take another example. Suppose you raise $10 million for your venture, but the investor gets a 1X liquidation preference and participation. His ownership percentage is 30%.

After a year, the company is sold for $20 million. The investor gets the $10 million back plus 30% of the remaining amount, or $3 million. The remaining $7 million goes to the rest of the shareholders.

As you can see, a participation clause can take a big bite from a transaction. As much as possible, try to eliminate it from the term sheet.

If this is not possible, try to get a cap. For example, you may agree that the amount of the liquidation preference and the participation may not exceed 2X the initial investment.

In the Series A stage, it's easy to get a sense of the impact of the liquidation preference and participation. But with Series B and subsequent rounds, the math can become complicated, because there will likely be multiple preferences and participations. Thus it's a good idea to have a spreadsheet to test the myriad alternatives. You do this by using a *capitalization table* (or *cap table* for short). It lists all the shareholders in a company and makes it easy to see how changes will impact the equity percentages. Your attorney should provide such a table.

Board of Directors

All C-Corps have a board of directors, which can range from three to ten members or so. They often meet every month or two to review the company's progress and weigh-in on strategic decisions.

But the board is more than a source of advice. It also has lots of power. Consider that it can appoint and fire the CEO. This is why VCs negotiate hard to get as much power as possible over the board seats.

Zuckerberg saw this as something to avoid at all costs. To realize his vision of a global powerhouse—which would involve holding back on advertising deals, saying no to mega-buyout offers from companies like Yahoo, and deferring an IPO—he knew that he had to maintain control of the board.

Zuckerberg also had the advantage of getting valuable advice from Sean Parker on the matter. Parker was kicked out of the company he founded, Plaxo, because he didn't have enough control over the board. And he also got kicked out of Napster!

To avoid this result at Facebook, Parker recommended that Zuckerberg set up the corporate governance to give him power to name three out of the five board seats. The other two went to Peter Thiel, who was known to be founder friendly, and Jim Breyer, a partner at Accel.

It wasn't until June 2008 that Zuckerberg made a move to elect an outside board member: Marc Andreessen. Back in the mid-1990s, Andreessen ignited the Internet revolution with the Netscape browser. Zuckerberg instantly confided in Andreessen because he had first-hand experience of the challenges of being a 20-something wunderkind.

Then, in March 2009, Zuckerberg brought on another key board member: Donald Graham, CEO of *The Washington Post*. They became good friends and shared a deep sense of the importance of creating a company that is built to last.

The lesson is not to rush things. Doing so only adds to the complexity and, even worse, to a loss of control. Spend time getting to know potential board members and developing a feel for their philosophies on major issues.

Some VCs may request an observer seat for board meetings. It's tempting to agree, because you won't lose any power. But you should still say "No." For the most part, an observer only adds to the distractions at board meetings.

In terms of compensation, a board member usually receives stock options instead of cash, as well as reimbursement for travel and out-of-pocket expenses. But be careful. The reimbursements must be *reasonable*. You don't want to pay for the gas in a VC's jet!

Anti-Dilution

A *down round* is horrible. This happens when the next series of funding is at a lower valuation. Existing shareholders usually take a hit, and employees and founders also feel lots of pain. It can be so bad that key people decide to leave, putting the venture in jeopardy.

A VC anticipates this possibility and puts in place protections known as *anti-dilution clauses*. The problem is that the founders and employees don't get these protections.

Even though this seems unfair, it doesn't matter. Anti-dilution clauses are standard features in a term sheet.

But there are ways to lessen the pain. To understand how, you need to know about the different types of anti-dilution clauses.

The most severe is the *full ratchet*, which triggers the issuance of new shares to an existing investor and reduces the price of the prior financing to the same price as the current round. The result is that the founders see massive dilution. If this occurs, it's best for a founder to leave. The down round will already have created a major loss in confidence, and the investors probably want you to leave anyway.

The other type of anti-dilution clause is the *weighted average approach*. It involves a convoluted equation that blends a lower price and new shares issued. Basically, it lessens the severity of the dilution's impact for the founders. The level depends on the formula, which has two flavors: broad-based and narrow-based. The math is beyond the scope of this book. But as a general rule, the broad-based approach is best for entrepreneurs. It still has a sting but is tolerable.

Pay-to-Play

For the most part, you want existing investors to participate in future rounds because it's a telling sign of their confidence in the company. It also helps to promote continuity. It cannot be stressed too much that your investors are key partners in your company's success.

To encourage future investments, you can include a play-to-play provision in the term sheet. If the investor doesn't invest, preferred stock converts into common stock. This means the investor loses key advantages, such as the liquidation preference and the anti-dilution clause.

You probably won't see a pay-to-play provision in the initial term sheet. It's up to you to bring it up and highlight how it's important to the deal. You can say something like, "Aren't you interested in the long-term prospects of the company? Why not invest in the future rounds?"

If there is still pushback, you need to reconsider the investor. Will they be there when times are tough?

A pay-to-play provision may not be appropriate for angels, though. They are using their personal funds and may not want to feel obligated to keep funding the company. Out of deference, you may want to leave such a provision out of the term sheet for the angel round.

Drag-Along

A drag-along provision requires founders and other key shareholders to vote in favor of a major corporate transaction, such as a sale or merger. It can make for a self-fulfilling prophesy. For example, suppose XYZ invests $10 million in ABC and has a 3X liquidation preference. Microsoft comes along and offers $20 million for the company. The VC wants to get a quick return for their portfolio—because their other investments have been lagging—and agrees to the deal. If there are drag-along rights, everyone else must do so as well. But the problem is that all the other shareholders will get nothing.

In other words, founders should negotiate this hard. Keep in mind that Zuckerberg didn't have a drag-along clause in his financings.

If you cannot knock out the clause completely, there are some ways to soften it. One is to require majority approval from the common stock holders. If investors complain, say that the preferred stock holders have the option to convert to common stock.

Another helpful clause is to require a minimum valuation on the deal. It could be something like 2X the liquidation preference.

Not-So-Important Clauses

Now let's look at clauses that are not essential. Although you should put up some resistance to them, you need not spend too much effort on it. Save your time for the clauses already discussed.

Conversion Rights

This clause involves the conversion of preferred stock into common stock. One approach is an optional conversion right, which gives a preferred stock holder the discretion of whether to convert their stock. Often this is done when maximizing the value from a liquidation preference.

Huh? To understand this, let's take an example. Suppose ABC invests $10 million in XYZ and gets 20%. The preferred stock has a 1X liquidation preference, but there is no participation.

After a few years, XYZ sells out to Facebook for $100 million. ABC gets only $10 million with the liquidation. Thus, a better option is to convert the preferred stock to get 20% in common stock, which amounts to $20 million (this is known as *on a converted basis*).

In some cases, there is a mandatory conversion right. This means a conversion takes place as a result of a certain event, which is typically an IPO. It's much cleaner for a public company to have only common stock.

A mandatory conversion has a threshold amount, which is the minimum that needs to be raised in the public offering. For a startup, it's important to set this threshold as low as possible. For example, if there is a conversation at $100 million, this may give an investor leverage to negotiate better terms or more equity. But if the amount was instead $20 million, the conversion would be automatic because most IPOs exceed this amount. In fact, if the amount is less than $50 million, you should not have much of a problem with the mandatory conversion clause.

Redemption Rights

Some companies are known as the "living dead," which means they have little growth potential. VCs don't have much opportunity to see outsized gains in such cases.

Yet they may want to get their money back. This can be done with a *redemption right* (or a *put*), which allows an investor to require a company to repurchase shares after a fixed period of time. Despite this, the redemption right may be useless because the company may not have enough cash on hand to buy back the shares.

If you cannot eliminate the redemption right in a term sheet, you should push back on the time limit—say, providing for five years or more. You should also not tie it to a "material adverse change" clause (this is when a major event happens, such as an earthquake or a terrorist incident). It's important to limit the redemption right to the initial investment amount, which doesn't include any dividends.

Dividends

A *dividend* is a distribution of cash from a company to its investors. It seems strange for a startup to have such a clause; dividends are supposed to come out of a company's profits, which probably don't exist for a startup.

Some dividends are *cumulative*. This means that if a dividend isn't paid, it accumulates in a reserve account. No other investor gets a payment until these dividends are paid off. You should definitely fight against cumulative dividends.

A *non-cumulative* dividend means a board must declare a dividend. If not, then there is no payment for the year. And yes, this is much better.

No Shop

From a legal standpoint, a term sheet is non-binding. Both parties can walk away from the deal at any point, without consequence.

Yet this isn't likely to happen. In the investing world, reputation is vitally important. A VC doesn't want to be known for leaving a company at the altar. At the same time, an entrepreneur doesn't want to be considered flaky. After all, they most likely need to keep raising money.

There are some provisions in a term sheet that a VC wants to make binding. One is the *no shop* clause. This forbids a founder from actively seeking out another term sheet after an agreement is reached.

The VC may try to set this at 90 days or more. But you should have a period no longer than 30 days.

Protective Provisions

These are veto rights for investors. It doesn't matter what the board says. A vote from the shareholders doesn't matter either. A protective provision always trumps everything else.

Certain standard provisions probably can't be negotiated away, such as the following:

- Sale of the company
- Amendments to the certificate of incorporation or the bylaws
- Changes in the total number of authorized preferred and common stock
- Issuances of new securities that have preferences over existing preferred stock
- Redemption of preferred shares or common stock
- Payment of a dividend or any cash distribution
- Change in the number of directors

But there are some you can probably push back on:

- Change in the focus of the business
- Hiring or firing of an executive
- Engaging in a transaction with an executive or a director
- Incurring debt over a certain limit

Registration Rights

For an early-stage company, this clause definitely is not worth negotiating. It sets forth the rights for the investors when there is a filing of an IPO, which probably won't happen for four to five years. Facebook didn't go public until eight years after its founding.

If the investors spend much time on registration rights, it's a sign that they don't understand the nuances of early-stage companies. In the end, the investor may not be appropriate for your company. Besides, do you want to eat up legal fees on something that is a non-issue?

Founder's Activities

Many entrepreneurs have outside business interests. These may include angel investments, side projects, or board seats.

Such activities are not necessarily problems. If anything, they are a good way to gain more experience and expand your contacts.

But some investors may be concerned about a founder's focus. Is the founder spending too much time on outside activities? Or may there be conflicts of interest?

A "Founder's Activities" clause sets some general guidelines. As with any negotiation, be up front and honest. If you plan to continue to engage in outside activities, make sure you disclose this to the investor. You don't want this to be a source of contention in the future, which could hurt the company and your relationship with the investor.

Resale Restrictions

Until recently, this clause didn't get much attention. But now it has become important because of the emergence of secondary markets like SecondMarket and SharesPost. These are online exchanges that allow investors and employees to sell their shares to outsiders even though the stock is not publicly traded.

A company may want to put restrictions on potential buyers. Do you want to have an employee sell shares to a competitor? Or what if they cash out a huge amount of stock and have little incentive to work for the venture? These are real concerns, and investors want to try to deal with them up front.

Perhaps the best way to do this is with a *resale restriction*—or the *right of first refusal (ROFR)*. It gives the company the right to buy shares at the current valuation. Or it can select its own buyer. This is something Facebook did; for example, one of the approved buyers was Digital Sky Ventures.

It's tough to negotiate a resale restriction. Then again, it's an effective way to help a company's growth by trying to avoid the disruption of unmanaged sales of securities.

A VC may also request a co-sale agreement. This means that if a founder wants to sell shares, other investors can do so as well. This is a standard clause and doesn't necessarily harm the company. Thus there is no reason to waste time negotiating it.

Information Rights

This clause shows who has the right to inspect the company's financials and other key disclosures. Investors always request this, and it's not a major negotiating problem. They deserve to understand the progress of their investment, right? Of course they do.

But there is a wrinkle. With the emergence of secondary markets, smaller outside investors may get shares. In this case, it's a good idea to limit their ability to gain access to sensitive information about the company.

Due Diligence

Once the term sheet is signed, the next step is to put together a variety of legal documents, such as the shareholder agreement. At the same time, the investors engage in a due diligence of your venture.

Due diligence is often fairly quick and straightforward for an early-stage company. There often isn't much operational history to scrutinize.

Despite this, you need to show your potential investors that you run a clean shop. Make sure all the company's affairs are in order. Some of the main things include having vesting of founder's stock, invention agreements, fully reviewed contracts, and a proper Delaware C-Corp.

The due-diligence process is intrusive and may feel uncomfortable. And yes, there are probably some things you don't want investors to know. But don't hide them. They will eventually come out. Hiding issues may not tank the financing, but it could create distrust and mean a lower valuation.

Summary

As you've seen in this chapter, the negotiating process for a funding is far from easy. It requires strong negotiating skills as well as an understanding of the key elements of a term sheet. Having a highly qualified team is a huge help.

The next chapter looks at something that often doesn't get enough attention: the go-to-market strategy. Even if you have the world's best product, it doesn't matter if your potential customers don't know about it!

Go-to-Market

Google actually relies on our users to help with our marketing. We have a very high percentage of our users who often tell others about our search engine.

—Sergey Brin

Your product can be a great sales tool as long as it is super-easy to use and provides instantly high value to users. They will usually spread the word about the product, creating more and more growth.

But there needs to be more. To reach breakout velocity, a company must solve the tricky issue of distribution. Yet many entrepreneurs devote too little attention to this subject.

Mark Zuckerberg has always understood the importance of distribution. All his apps have involved some level of sharing, which helped greatly to spread their adoption.

Zuckerberg also used creative approaches to supercharge growth. One ingenious strategy—which cost virtually nothing—was to allow new members to import the contacts from their Hotmail, Yahoo!, and Gmail accounts. Facebook also created profiles for users who had not even signed up—called *dark profiles*—that were based on tagged photos. It was another way to help make it easier for those people to become real members. All these efforts had a cumulative impact, making it possible to end-run rivals like MySpace.

This chapter looks at some of the main strategies you can use to boost distribution of your product. This doesn't mean you should use all of them or even a few of them. Keep in mind that products often have one prime distribution mechanism. It will likely take some experimentation to figure out the optimal approach for your situation.

Two Types of Markets

Back in 2005, Chan Kim and Renée Mauborgne published the path-breaking book *Blue Ocean Strategy* (Harvard Business Review Press, 2005). The premise was that huge opportunities exist to create new markets that have little competition and customers with significant unmet needs. One of the examples in the book is Cirque du Soleil. By blending elements of opera, ballet, and the circus, the company was able to create a new, highly profitable category.

Facebook is also an example of a blue ocean opportunity. Although it was not the first player in the social-networking space, it was the one that got two critical things right. The first was timing. Facebook came at a point when the world was ready for a way to create an online identity and openly share status updates, photos, and videos with friends. Facebook also realized that it was critically important to focus on a few key features, which included the News Feed, tagging photos, and the developer platform.

When a company effectively executes on a blue ocean strategy, the results can be astounding. The company almost doesn't need a go-to-market strategy because word of mouth catapults it into the stratosphere. This is why Peter Thiel's famous advice to Zuckerberg during the early days was, "Just don't f**k it up."

The problem is that blue ocean opportunities are exceedingly rare. The typical scenario is instead to attack an existing market, which is usually dominated by several entrenched players.

How does a tiny company pull off a David-and-Goliath move? You need to come up with a way to disrupt the market. And yes, this has been set forth in another game-changing book: Clayton Christensen's *The Innovator's Dilemma* (Harvard Business Review Press, 1997). His playbook is fairly straightforward. It involves focusing on the low end of a market, which the major operators don't care about. An upstart company can use agility and innovation to make the market profitable. This can then be a launching pad to move into higher-end segments.

An example is Yelp. Co-founders Jeremy Stoppelman and Russel Simmons firmly believed that the multibillion-dollar Yellow Pages business was vulnerable to disruption. But it needed an innovation to upend the market. As the founders studied the landscape, they realized that customers relied on referrals from trusted people when going to a restaurant or selecting a service provider. So why not allow anyone to post reviews on a web site?

It was a big idea, but Yelp did not immediately set out to create a national platform. The founders wanted to start in San Francisco and focus on the nightclub scene. The approach was something the Yellow Pages industry considered a waste of time with little profit potential. But for Yelp, the move allowed it to refine its business and build a solid foundation.

Keep in mind that it took Yelp a few years to get traction as the Yellow Pages industry began taking notice. This is typical for market disruptions, because it is painstakingly difficult to get consumers to change their habits, even if the new approach is far superior. To push things forward, the founder needs to constantly talk about the mission—and decry the evils of the incumbents. But in the end, it can be an effective way to create a billion-dollar company.

The rest of this chapter looks at some go-to-market strategies that can help you, whether your company is pursuing a blue ocean opportunity or a play to disrupt a market. But before diving in, let's first look at the fundamentals of marketing. They're crucial if you want to build an enduring company.

Key Marketing Metrics

During the dot-com boom of the 1990s, companies used a large amount of their capital for marketing. Companies like Pets.com sponsored major events, advertised aggressively across the Web, and even produced Super Bowl commercials. Although these efforts resulted in massive traffic, they proved to be inherently unprofitable. When the venture capital markets shut down, thousands of dot-coms evaporated.

It's true that marketing is not an exact science and that there will certainly be wasteful expenditures. But startups can use some basic concepts to improve the odds of success.

At the core is understanding how to measure things. One metric is the customer lifetime value (CLV), which involves measuring the average revenue per user, the gross profit, and the average customer churn. Changes in any of these variables can have a big impact on your business, although the most significant is likely to be the average customer churn. If there is new competition or the product is languishing, you may see deep attrition in your customer base, and this can wreck your business.

Thus companies need to spend time on programs to improve retention. This means being responsive to customer needs as well as continuing to invest in the product.

The amount of the CLV ranges based on the industry. For a consumer Internet site, the CLV may be low—say, under $100. On the other hand, for some businesses the CLV is enormous, perhaps in the millions. This is typically the case for enterprise software companies.

Once you have a reasonable grasp of the CLV, you need to measure the cost to acquire a customer (CAC). It consists mostly of advertising and marketing costs.

For a company to be successful, the CLV must exceed the CAC. Speed is also critical; you should recoup your CAC within about 12 months. Doing so is a sign that a company has a strong business model and should eventually see healthy profitability.

One of the top players in understanding the CLV/CAC dynamic is Zynga. In the early days, the company already had games that were addictive and viral, spreading through users' News Feeds on Facebook. But Zynga's CEO, Mark Pincus, wanted to make his company the category leader—and this meant finding ways to boost distribution. With his rounds of funding, he invested heavily in building a core infrastructure that made it easy to test and measure the impact of online marketing. He also hired some of the industry's top online marketing pros.

With a clear-cut understanding of each game's CLV/CAC profile, Pincus was able to profitably grow Zynga at lightning speed. It turned out to be a huge advantage that his competitors could not match.

Keep in mind that a company's CAC is one of the largest expense items on a profit and loss (P&L) statement, if not the largest. Because of this, VCs want to see that you have thought about low-cost approaches to marketing and advertising. Some of the common strategies include partnerships, viral distribution, search-engine optimization, meetups, PR, and, yes, the use of celebrities. Let's look at each in more detail.

Partnerships

When you look back at some of history's legendary companies, an early partnership often propelled distribution. A classic example is Microsoft, which teamed up with IBM in the early 1980s to provide the operating system for the PC. The relationship made DOS a global standard, which led to tremendous cash flows. These financed other franchise products like Windows and Office. Eventually, Microsoft was worth more than IBM.

Another example is Google. It always had its own destination site, but the distribution strategy was to strike partnerships with portals. A critical deal was made with Yahoo!, which allowed Google to refine its search algorithms at scale. The company also got lots of exposure because the search page was co-branded. And yes, Google was eventually worth more than Yahoo!.

So, partnerships should be a major consideration for any startup. They may be indispensable for success.

Yet they must have a strategic purpose. Before seeking out partnerships, you need to think hard about which companies would be your ideal partners. This means doing extensive research on the market so you understand which companies have the most promising futures.

The next step is to make it as easy as possible to get a partner on board. Consider that it can take months—if not years—to get a deal done. Large companies are often resistant to spending time and resources dealing with a small operator.

To help accelerate the process, you should create your infrastructure to make integrating a partner straightforward. This is much easier nowadays thanks to application programming interfaces (APIs), which are code modules that allow third parties to hook into a web site or a mobile app. But an API is more than just good coding. It must be easy to use and, most important, it must not fail. Big companies are risk averse and don't want to jeopardize their hard-won reputations.

Even with a strong API, there are still challenges. To land a mega-partner, you need to be persistent and find the decision-makers in the organization with which you wish to partner. You also must to be prepared to make a standout presentation that addresses the risks and shows the immediate opportunities. If you can demonstrate that a partnership will create new revenues, your chances of success increase greatly.

One of the masters of creating partnerships was Steve Case, who turned AOL into the dot-com era's version of Facebook. When he merged the company with Time-Warner in 2000, the combined value was over $350 billion.

But in the early days of AOL, there were other major players in the market, such as IBM and CompuServe. To be a winner, Case realized that partnerships would be important in supercharging his growth. And he saw Apple as a key.

Case went from Virginia to Cupertino, California and lived in a hotel for months while trying to form a partnership with Apple. He vowed not to leave until he had a deal. In the end, his determination paid off, and the Apple relationship turned out to be critical for AOL's success.

Despite all this, partnerships are not cure-alls. The dependency can prove fatal for a company. There are many examples, such as what happened with LookSmart. A pioneering online search engine, the company relied on

Microsoft for its distribution. The problem was that LookSmart did not seek out ways to diversify its revenues. By 2003, Microsoft accounted for a whopping 65% of revenues. As online search marketing became more profitable, as demonstrated by the growth of Google, Microsoft wanted its own platform. As a result, the company did not renew the partnership agreement, and LookSmart's stock price collapsed. Since then, it has not been able to recover.

Viral Distribution

All distribution strategies have a cost, but the expenditure for one is extremely low: viral marketing. In fact, the cost is often near zero. The reason is that your users get other users to join.

When a product is viral, growth is usually explosive, and the company almost inevitably becomes a mega-player. Examples include Hotmail, Skype, YouTube, Dropbox, and, yes, Facebook.

To determine whether a product is viral, you need to understand the *viral coefficient*, which shows the conversion rate of a user to the number of invites. For example, suppose a person signs up and invites ten friends. With a conversion rate of 15%, the viral coefficient is 1.5. Keep in mind that if it's greater than 1, you probably have a viral product.

But you need something else: a quick conversion cycle. If it takes six months for a user to send out invites, then your product won't reach breakout velocity. For a truly viral product, users need to send out invites within 24 hours of signing up.

The problem is that few products are viral. But don't despair: there are things you can do to bring viral magic to your product. One of the simplest approaches is to place buttons on your site that allow users to send messages to their friends via Twitter or Facebook. This is a no-brainer.

Or you may want to provide rewards for referrals. This has been the case with Dropbox, which provides free storage for each new user who joins. It's a great incentive and has resulted in a huge number of sign-ups. Dropbox now has more than 50 million users.

You may even want to try non-automated approaches, which is what Pandora has done. The company's product is not necessarily viral, but its growth rate has been staggering. Of course, it was smart that Pandora developed a mobile product in the early days of smartphones. It also has a great service that delivers songs based on what a user likes. But Pandora has gone even further.

When you sign up, you get an e-mail from the personal account of co-founder Tim Westergren. If you respond, you get an answer! This has been a highly effective way to turn users into rabid fans.

After all, when you sign up for a new service, you often get a message that says something like, "Don't respond to this e-mail." What kind of way is that to treat a customer?

When using viral marketing techniques, you need to avoid any inkling of spam. Users are becoming increasingly intolerant of these dubious tactics. Such approaches get tweeted about and may end up as part of an exposé story by a blogger. Always make it clear what you plan to do with any information from a user. And if you send out e-mail alerts or newsletters, they should be opt-in.

Search Engine Optimization (SEO)

SEO has become a huge business over the past decade. The idea is that by producing lots of relevant content, your site's links should rise to the top of search listings for Google, Bing, and Yahoo!.

But this isn't easy to pull off, and some companies push the boundaries beyond ethics and decency. Because of this, search engines are becoming more diligent about preventing SEO spam. These efforts can actually shut down a company.

Also be wary of third-party SEO consulting firms. They make grandiose promises but don't necessarily deliver. Or they may engage in shady practices.

Despite all this, SEO is a great way to get free distribution for your product. The key is that the content must be authentic and relevant—not an attempt to try to game the system.

It also helps if the business relies on heavy amounts of user-generated content. This is certainly the case with Yelp. Its users have created over 25 million reviews, which has caused Yelp merchant profiles to rank high on online searchers.

When entering a new city, Yelp hires a community manager who is a local resident. The manager writes a weekly e-mail and organizes events. These efforts are essential in getting users to write lots of useful reviews.

This extra step—having "feet on the street"—is often lacking in startups. Somehow the belief is that the users will automatically start contributing content. But this is often a false hope. To be successful, it is usually critical that you engage in proactive actions.

Meetups

Meetups can be extremely helpful in getting exposure for your product. They aren't hard to put together and aren't necessarily expensive. You can have a meetup at a nice hotel, with free drinks.

Don't expect to get an immediate spike in users after a meetup. Keep in mind that the people who attend meetups are probably already avid users.

But this is an advantage: the event can be a way to maintain intensity as well as an opportunity to get feedback and ideas about possible features. Requesting such input will impress your avid users, and they may tell more of their friends about your product. Such word-of-mouth marketing can be powerful.

At a meetup, it's a good idea to have giveaways. At a minimum, you should provide t-shirts—your users can become walking billboards for your company. Raffle something like an iPad. And make sure you take pictures of the event and post them on your company's blog as well as your Twitter and Facebook pages.

It's important to follow up with all the people who attend the meetup. Say thanks, and ask for feedback.

Now: what about launch parties, which seem to be *de rigueur* in Silicon Valley? I consider them a waste of money. They're really just a way for people to throw a free party! In the end, you probably won't get much lift in your user base. Meetups, on the other hand, offer a better opportunity to reach more people at a much cheaper price.

PR

PR is critical for any company. It is the best kind of exposure because you are getting an unbiased view from a third party. In today's skeptical world, this can be huge when you are trying to acquire users and customers.

But here's the problem: it's not easy to get good PR exposure. There aren't many influential blogs and publications. Thus there aren't many reporters and bloggers—at least, compared to the thousands of startups looking for coverage.

As a blogger for Forbes.com, I have some insights that can help with your PR efforts. Much of my advice is simple. For example, you need a News section on your web site. When I visit a company's site, this is the first place I go; before I write about the company, I want to see who else has covered it and learn about the key points that set it apart from the crowd. Unfortunately, the

News section often contains little useful information (if the section even exists!).

A company should also devote some effort to its own blog. Write about the latest developments, especially major partnerships and customers, and try to show that your company has real traction.

It's also good for your CEO to post regularly. But don't make these posts solely about the company's products. The CEO should blog about pressing issues in the industry. If your CEO becomes a thought leader, this may lead to more PR opportunities. Remember, bloggers like to quote experts.

Before you pitch a blogger, you need to read their stuff. Nothing is more aggravating than getting a pitch that concerns something I've never written about. Do you expect me to suddenly start covering something new? It's not going to happen. Such a pitch shows that a company gave little thought to the effort.

Also, from time to time I receive a PR e-mail that has been messed up by the mass e-mailer. When I get a pitch that starts with

Hi {Name}

it's an automatic delete for me.

When pitching your company, get to the point. Avoid sending an e-mail that goes on *ad nauseam*. Reporters don't have time to read treatises. Keep your pitches to no more than a couple of paragraphs. You may even want to paste in a screen shot that gives a good idea of the product.

To boost your odds of getting the attention of a reporter or blogger, you need to provide a *hook*: a nugget that is interesting to readers. An example is a pitch I got that—in the subject line—mentioned "the power of the hoodie." It was in reference to Zuckerberg's attire during the IPO roadshow. I loved the phrase; it was interesting enough that I contacted the PR person. In the end, I wound up writing a story on the topic.

Sometimes, founders need to restrain themselves. To get publicity, it's tempting to stretch the truth or even lie. It's okay to be optimistic—that's mandatory for an entrepreneur—but you need to act with integrity. In today's world, it's often easy to spot untruths.

Just because a reporter responds to a pitch, this doesn't mean a story is inevitable. Sometimes a writer is only making an introductory call and getting your company on their radar. But a response is a good sign; chances are, the writer will cover your company at some point.

What if a blogger writes a negative piece? Your first instinct may be to lash out. But you need to control yourself. If the story contains a glaring error or misrepresentation, get in touch with the blogger and point it out. But again, don't be hostile—that will probably make things worse.

Negative media coverage is inevitable, especially for successful companies. In the early days of Facebook, the reporting was far from glowing. It was common to see pieces about how the site was a fad and a terrible violator of privacy. But in reality, the media attention was a good thing. It showed that Facebook was interesting to readers, which gave writers a reason to keep writing about it. Zuckerberg quickly realized this and did not fight back against negative coverage. It took a strong stomach but was definitely the winning strategy.

The Celebrity Factor

Some types of businesses can benefit tremendously from being associated with celebrities. Keep in mind that getting adopted by Hollywood stars was a key fuel for Twitter's growth. This was also a factor for Facebook.

If your venture is focused on the consumer side—especially if it's in fashion or entertainment—try to get celebrities on board. This has happened with various companies that have had success connecting with Shakira, Will Smith, Rihanna, Jay-Z, and Snoop Dogg.

And of course, Ashton Kutcher has become an Internet tycoon by taking advantage of his celebrity. His star power has been a key driver for the success of companies like Fab.com.

Summary

This chapter just scratched the surface of the possible go-to-market strategies. It's a highly specialized topic. In fact, one of your early hires should be an expert in marketing.

The next chapter looks at financial matters. These can be a bit boring, but you need to know the core principles. This means understanding the income statement, balance sheet, and cash flow statement. They are important in guiding the early success of your company.

The Financials

In the end, all business operations can be reduced to three words: people, product, and profits.

—Lee Iacocca

A key to Facebook is its focus on data. From the early days, Mark Zuckerberg made it a priority to develop systems that tracked numerous metrics such as daily active users, time spent on the site, mobile traffic, and so on.

But in order for the data to have any meaning, it must be connected to the financials. Toward this end, Zuckerberg has also focused on creating a highly sophisticated financial reporting system. This has made it easier to monetize traffic and also to meet the rigorous compliance requirements of being a public company. This is why Zuckerberg had to learn how to interpret financial statements and understand important concepts like margins.

This chapter covers these things—by analyzing Facebook's own financials.

Accounting Fundamentals

The basics of accounting go all the way back to Renaissance Italy. At the time, Luca Pacioli came up with the system of double-entry bookkeeping, with the premise that every transaction needed two equal components. Here's a modern-day example. If you buy a server for your company, you increase the asset amount on your financial statements but also decrease the cash balance by the same amount. Why? To help avoid accounting errors. If the two columns don't balance, there is definitely something wrong.

Since Pacioli's time, the accounting profession has seen much evolution. Just look at the case of Zynga. The company innovated a business model that involves selling virtual items for its social games. But no guidelines existed for how to account for the revenues. Do you recognize them when a purchase is made or ratably over the period a player is engaged in the game? To resolve this issue, Zynga had to use its best judgment and also get the help of its auditors.

A critical part of accounting are Generally Accepted Accounting Principles (GAAP). These include an extensive set of accounting guidelines that have been developed by authorities like the Securities and Exchange Commission, the American Institute of Certified Public Accountants (AICPA), the Financial Accounting Standards Board (FASB), and the Public Company Accounting Oversight Board (PCAOB).

When a company goes public, it's required to report its financials in accordance with GAAP. But it has the option to add other measures, called *pro forma metrics*, which are at the discretion of management. As should be no surprise, the temptation is to be extremely liberal so as to inflate the company's profitability.

A common metric is earnings before interest, taxes, depreciation, and amortization (EBITDA). There may also be variations, known as *adjusted* EBITDA. The rationale is that certain items should be excluded from earnings because they are not part of the main operations of a company (such as interest) or don't involve a current outlay of cash (depreciation).

But these accounting games are unfortunate. Why does management need to resort to such shenanigans, especially when professional investors can see what's really going on? Perhaps one of the most notable examples of using pro forma numbers is Groupon. In its S-1 filing, the company highlighted its own accounting invention: adjusted consolidated segment operating income (adjusted CSOI). Besides being a mouthful, it turned into a major controversy with IPO investors. Adjusted CSOI excluded marketing and customer-acquisition costs, even though these expenditures were critical to the company's business model!

The SEC ultimately required Groupon to underemphasize this metric in its S-1. After the company came public, it wound up having to restate its first quarter earnings report, which was a major embarrassment. The stock lost as much as 70% of its value.

Facebook took another approach. When it filed for its IPO, the company didn't resort to fancy metrics. Instead, it published clean GAAP numbers, which made it easy for investors to understand things and helped to bolster credibility. It also allowed for a smooth approval process with the SEC.

For startups, being creative is crucial in building a breakout company. But it's a terrible strategy when it comes to accounting.

Conservativism

For the most part, accounting principles emphasize conservative approaches. One is the concept of *historical cost*. To understand this, let's take an example. If Facebook buys a server, it must book this at its cost, even if the company bought the server at well below its worth. It doesn't matter.

But the historical cost approach can be misleading. Let's say Facebook purchased land for its headquarters five years ago for $10 million. With the surge in prices, it's now worth $13 million. Despite this, Facebook cannot increase the value of the property on its financials. The land must remain at its historical cost. This is a hard-line rule.

Another important accounting principle is the *accrual method*. This has two parts, but they are intertwined. First, a company must recognize revenues when they're earned, not when cash is paid. If Facebook has generated $1 million in sales from Zynga, it's a sale even though the payment won't be made until the end of the month.

Second, a company must recognize expenses when they're incurred, not when cash is paid. Again, let's say Facebook agrees to buy software for $500,000. At this moment, it's an expense.

This seems convoluted, but there is a rationale. It's part of something called the *matching principle,* which says a company must report all expenses that relate to revenues. Doing so makes it easier to get a sense of the company's overall progress.

Without the matching principle, financials would often be mess. Just imagine if Facebook prepaid rent for six months. Would it make sense to recognize the entire expense for the current month? Definitely not. Doing so would give a false impression. The proper way is for Facebook to recognize the expense over the six-month period as it uses the property.

Income Statement

The income statement starts with revenues and then subtracts costs. The result is either a profit or a loss. Although profitability is not a consideration for early-stage companies, it's a key factor when a company scales its growth and especially when it comes public. Facebook posted a profit of $1 billion in 2011, which compares to only $229 million in 2009.

An income statement covers activity for a period of time, such as a quarter or a year. Facebook's income statement provided a break-out for 2009 to 2011 and then the first quarter of 2011 and 2012, as shown in Table 8-1.

Table 8-1. Facebook's Income Statements

	Year Ended December 31,			Three Months Ended March 31,	
	2009	**2010**	**2011**	**2011**	**2012**
(in millions, except per share data)					
Revenue	$777	$1,974	$3,711	$731	$1,058
Costs and expenses:					
Cost of revenue	223	493	860	167	277
Marketing and sales	115	184	427	68	159
Research and development	87	144	388	57	153
General and administrative	90	121	280	51	88
Total costs and expenses	515	942	1,955	343	677
Income from operations	262	1,032	1,756	398	382
Interest and other income (expense), net	(8)	(24)	(61)	10	1
Income before provision for income taxes	254	1,008	1,695	398	382
Provision for income taxes	25	402	695	165	177
Net income	229	606	1,000	233	205
Earnings per share					
Basic	0.12	0.34	0.52	0.12	0.10
Diluted	0.10	0.28	0.46	0.11	0.09

When you look at this table, notice that the numbers are in millions, which makes them easy to interpret. You also see that some numbers are surrounded by brackets; these are negative numbers.

Now let's take a deeper look at the items on the income statement.

Revenue

Revenues or *sales* refer to the total amount a company receives from selling products or providing services. This is also called the *top line* because it's listed at the top of the statement. In some cases, you see *Net Sales*, which excludes certain items from gross sales like discounts, promotions, and returns.

Facebook gets about 82% of its revenues from advertising and the rest from fees resulting from its Credits platform, which provides payment services (mostly for social gaming partners like Zynga). From 2010 to 2011, the number of users for virtual goods went from 5 million to 15 million.

Even though Facebook is available in most countries, it still gets a majority of its revenues from the US. The other main sources include Western Europe, Canada, and Australia. It takes considerable time and resources to set up the infrastructure to monetize a web site in another country; this is why revenues are low in areas like India. Even though traffic has been growing at a rapid clip, there is little infrastructure to deliver ads. But over the next few years, Facebook will make the necessary investments to capitalize on the massive revenue opportunities.

It's also important to understand that revenue can be subject to seasonality. This means some quarters are stronger than others due to factors such as weather, budget decisions, and industry customs. In 2012, Facebook noted that it had a relatively weak first quarter because of seasonality. For most ad-based companies, this time period often sees the lowest activity.

This may have not been a problem in prior years because Facebook was growing at a torrid pace. But as it reached $4 billion in revenue, it appeared that seasonality was becoming a reality. It's natural as a company begins to mature and its growth rate slows.

Cost of Revenue

The cost of revenue includes all expenses that are directly related to the delivery of a company's products. For Facebook, these include the costs for data centers, equipment, bandwidth, energy, processing fees, and maintenance.

Of these, energy has been tough to control. This is why Facebook has situated data centers near electric power plants or in cold climates, because it is expensive to cool down servers

Gross Profit

This is revenues minus the cost of revenue. Investors analyze this number using the gross profit margin:

Gross Profit / Revenues

You want to see this above 50% because that means your company has much more room to be profitable. Facebook's gross margin was 73.4% by the first quarter of 2012, which was standout.

It's important for gross margins to increase over time, which indicates leverage in the business model. Again, it's a key source of profitability—which can drive massive valuations. This has been the case with companies like Microsoft and Google. And this is why VCs often talk about gross margins.

Marketing and Sales

There has never been a Facebook Super Bowl commercial—or any Facebook television commercial, for that matter. Because of its mega-brand and global reach, the company has had little need to engage in large-scale marketing efforts, except for sponsoring conferences and events. This has been a huge advantage that has helped the company post strong profits.

On the sales side, Facebook has built a self-service ad platform, which has also been a cost saver. But the company has had to ramp up the hiring of top sales and business-development people as well as customer representatives. Top-notch brands aren't satisfied with automated ad systems; they instead want the counsel of smart people who can create compelling campaigns. For this reason, Facebook has 30 sales offices around the globe.

Research and Development

This item consists mostly of salaries, benefits, and share-based compensation for engineers and computer scientists. Facebook has been aggressively hiring not just product-development people but also those with experience in areas like data mining and personalization technologies, content delivery, media storage and serving, power distribution, and advertising technologies.

These people are not cheap. In some cases, a top engineer commands a multi-million-dollar pay package.

As a result, R&D expenditures have increased substantially for Facebook. From 2009 to 2011, the costs went from $87 million to $388 million.

General and Administrative

These are known as *overhead* costs. That is, they tend to remain the same regardless of overall sales, at least in the short run. G&A costs include functions like finance, legal, and HR.

Net Income

This is a company's *bottom line* (yes, because it's at the bottom of the income statement). A positive number is a profit, and a negative number is a loss. A company calculates its earnings per share (EPS):

Net Income / Outstanding Shares

The outstanding shares can be those that are already owned. Or it can be on a diluted basis, which assumes that all options and warrants are exercised. Because fast-growing tech companies usually see high levels of exercises, it's better to focus on the diluted figure.

Once you have the EPS, you can find the price-to-earnings (PE) ratio:

Stock Price / EPS

This is a rough guide to a company's valuation. As a general rule, a hot tech company has a high PE ratio—say over 30 or 40—because investors pay a premium for growth. But it can also mean the stock is volatile. Even a small drop in the growth rate can hurt a stock. This has happened with public companies such as Zynga, Groupon, Yelp, and Pandora.

There are many flaws with the PE ratio, though. Perhaps the biggest is that it's backward-looking: it's based on the past 12 months of earnings. So, investors may instead use a forward PE ratio:

Price / Earnings Forecast for the Next 12 Months

And if a company has losses—which is common for tech companies—then these metrics are meaningless. What to do? Investors instead often look at the price-to-sales ratio:

Market Capitalization / Sales

The *market capitalization* (or *market cap*) is the stock price times the number of shares outstanding. It's essentially the total value of the company.

The price-to-sale ratio is a good way to compare the value of one company to another. For example, if Groupon has a ratio of 5 and LivingSocial's is 3, then Groupon is commanding a premium valuation.

Of course, Wall Street looks at other metrics as well. But for the most part, they focus on earnings and revenue growth. Because of this, a publicly traded tech company often announces its earnings and revenue forecasts for the next quarter and the full year. This helps to reduce volatility in the stock price because investors have a better sense of the company's momentum. Wall Street hates surprises.

But some companies like Facebook and Google don't provide any guidance. Their belief is that they should be focused on long-term growth, not quarter-by-quarter results. This approach is fairly rare on Wall Street; only marquee companies can do it.

The Balance Sheet

The balance sheet includes a company's assets, liabilities, and equity. It should always balance according to this equation:

Assets = Liabilities + Equity

This makes intuitive sense because to buy assets, a company needs to raise capital by obtaining loans or selling stock. The equity also includes retained earnings, which are profits. It's another key source for buying assets.

Tech companies like Facebook tend to be asset-light. Most of the value comes from supersmart engineers and the code they create—but they can't be listed as assets on a balance sheet. Although Facebook has total assets of $7.1 billion, the company's market value is over $50 billion.

Think of a balance sheet as a snapshot of a company at a certain point in time. It usually tallies everything at the end of the quarter, as you can see with Facebook's balance sheet in Table 8-2.

Table 8-2. Facebook's Balance Sheets

	December 31,		March 31,
	2010	**2011**	**2012**
Current assets:			
Cash and cash equivalents	1,785	1,512	1,282
Marketable securities		2,396	2,628
Accounts receivable	373	547	482
Prepaid expenses and other current assets	88	149	302
Property and equipment, net	574	1,475	1,855
Goodwill and intangible assets, net	96	162	189
Other assets	74	90	121

Total assets	2,990	6,331	6,859
Liabilities and stockholders' equity			
Current liabilities			
Accounts payable	29	63	129
Platform partners payable	75	171	178
Accrued expenses and other current liabilities	137	296	337
Deferred revenue and deposits	42	90	93
Current portion of capital lease obligations	106	279	302
Total current liabilities	389	899	1,039
Capital lease obligations	117	398	404
Long-term debt	250		
Other liabilities	72	135	144
Total liabilities	828	1,432	1,587
Stockholders' equity			
Convertible preferred stock	615	615	615
Common stock			
Additional paid-in capital	947	2,684	2,853
Accumulated other comprehensive loss	(6)	(6)	(7)
Retained earnings	606	1,606	1,811
Total stockholders' equity	2,162	4,899	5,272
Total liabilities and stockholders' equity	2,990	6,331	6,859

Let's take a look at the key items of the balance sheet.

Assets

An *asset* is anything a company owns, such as cash, inventory, or real estate. On a balance sheet, assets are listed in terms of *liquidity*, which is how quickly they can be converted into cash. The current assets can be turned into cash within a year or so.

Cash and Cash Equivalents, and Marketable Securities

A large company like Facebook keeps a relatively small amount of its cash in deposits. Instead, it holds marketable securities, such as Treasuries. These are near-cash but pay somewhat higher yields. The yield can be a big deal for a company like Facebook, which has high cash balances.

Accounts Receivable

An *account receivable* means a company has sold a product or service but the customer has yet to pay. This is actually an asset.

It's possible for a company to factor or sell accounts receivable, which can be a source of cash. Doing so is common for early-stage companies, but it can be expensive because the fees tend to be steep.

Also keep in mind that a few customers simply fail to pay. It's part of doing business (and it's never fun to deal with). Because of this, a company estimates a total for these losses, which is called the *allowance for doubtful accounts*.

Prepaid Assets

Prepaid assets are those items for which a company makes advance purchases. To understand this, let's take an example. Suppose Facebook prepays for five months of rent. It can recognize only one-fifth of this amount for the current month as an expense on the income statement. The rest is considered a prepaid asset.

Property and Equipment

According to GAAP, a company must depreciate property and equipment (but not land). This means it needs to reduce the value of the assets due to wear and tear and obsolescence.

A common approach is *straight-line depreciation*. This involves deducting an equal percentage periodically over the useful life of the asset. How long? It depends on the type of asset. This is what Facebook has:

- *Network equipment:* 3 to 4 years
- *Computer software and office equipment:* 2 to 5 years

- *Buildings:* 15 to 20 years

Let's say Facebook buys network equipment for $100,000. If it uses a four-year term, then the depreciation is $25,000 per year.

A company may also use other depreciation methods that accelerate the process. These may take 25% or more of the value of the property in the first or second year. For the most part, these approaches are based on various tax incentives.

Goodwill

Goodwill is the value from an acquisition: the purchase price minus the net asset value of the target company. Goodwill is fairly common in the tech world.

Suppose Facebook decides to pay $10 million for a mobile app company that has $1 million in net assets. The $9 million is accounted for as goodwill and considered an asset on the balance sheet.

To be in accordance with GAAP, goodwill must be tested at least once per year for *impairments* (this is the duty of an outside auditor). This is a fancy way of saying that an asset has lost value, such as from lower revenues or obsolescence. When there is an impairment, a company will need to take a loss.

Liabilities and Stockholders' Equity

A startup probably doesn't have much debt. Banks generally avoid early-stage ventures because there is no collateral to lend against.

But there are still some liabilities. One form is *accounts payable*, which is money owed to vendors. As a company grows, so do these liabilities. It's a key reason a startup needs to keep raising capital—and Facebook was no exception.

Statement of Cash Flows

Cash is king. It definitely makes a founder's life easier because it tends to mean much higher valuations and less pressure to raise outside capital.

EBITDA is often used as a proxy for a company's cash flows, but it's a crude approximation. A better approach is to use the statement of cash flows.

Table 8-3 shows the statement for Facebook.

Table 8-3. Facebook's Cash Flow Statements

Statement of Cash Flows					
	2009	**2010**	**2011**	**Three months ended March 31, 2011**	**Three months ended March 31, 2012**
Cash flows from operating activities					
Net income	$229	$606	$1,000	$233	$205
Adjustments to reconcile net income to net cash provided by operating activities					
Depreciation and amortization	78	139	323	51	110
Loss on write-off of assets	1	3	4	1	1
Share-based compensation	27	20	217	7	103
Tax benefit from share-based award activity	50	115	433	69	54
Excess tax benefit from share-based award activity	(51)	(115)	(433)	(69)	(54)
Changes in assets and liabilities					
Accounts receivable	(112)	(209)	(174)	27	65
Prepaid expenses and other current assets	(30)	(38)	(31)	(26)	(28)
Other assets	(59)	17	(32)	(10)	(32)
Accounts payable	(7)	12	6	(3)	(3)
Platform partners payable		75	96	24	7
Accrued expenses and other current liabilities	27	20	38	6	2
Deferred revenue and deposits	1	37	49	17	3
Other liabilities	1	16	53	18	8
Net cash provided by operating activities	155	698	1,549	345	441

Cash flows from investing activities

Purchases of property and equipment	(33)	(293)	(606)	(153)	(453)
Purchases of marketable securities			(3,025)		(876)
Maturities of marketable securities			516		567
Sales of marketable securities			113		69
Investments in non-marketable equity securities			(3)		(1)
Acquisitions of business, net of cash acquired, and purchases of intangible and other assets	3	(22)	(24)	(1)	(25)
Change in restricted cash and deposits	(32)	(9)	6	1	(1)
Net cash used in investing activities	(62)	(324)	(3,023)	(153)	(720)

Cash flows from financing activities

Net proceeds from issuance of convertible preferred stock	200				
Net proceeds from issuance of common stock		500	998	998	
Proceeds from exercise of stock options	9	6	28	9	5
Proceeds from (repayment of) long-term debt		250	(250)	(250)	
Proceeds from sale and lease-back transactions	31		170	1	62
Principal payments on capital lease obligations	(48)	(90)	(181)	(29)	(71)
Excess tax benefit from share-based award activity	51	115	433	69	54
Net cash provided by financing activities	243	781	1,198	798	50

Effect of exchange rate changes on cash and cash equivalents		(3)	3	1	(1)
Net increase (decrease) in cash and cash equivalents	336	1,152	(273)	991	(230)
Cash and cash equivalents at beginning of period	633	1,785	1,512	2,776	1,282

The statement includes adjustments for a variety of items on the income statement and balance sheet. Notice that there are three main sections, outlined next.

Cash Flows from Operating Activities

This shows Facebook's cash flows from its operating business. The section begins with net income, which is then adjusted for a variety of items. This involves adding back non-cash amounts—such as depreciation, amortization, and share-based compensation—to the net income. Then other items must be subtracted. A key item is accounts receivable, because Facebook has yet to receive any cash.

Cash Flows from Investing Activities

It's common to confuse the Investing section with the Financing section. But they have clear differences.

The Investing section includes major purchases, usually capital expenditures for assets that should last longer than a year. But these purchases reduce cash flows. At the same time, any sales of assets increase cash flows.

Over the years, Facebook has substantially increased its investment in capital assets to allow for its strong growth.

Cash Flows from Financing Activities

This is where a company includes inflows from issuing stock and debt. Of course, any buybacks or dividends are subtracted.

For tech companies, the Financing section is a huge source of cash. But over time, the company needs to show that it can generate positive operating cash flows. If not, it's a sign that the business model is flawed.

Summary

This chapter covered lots of ground and provided enough information for most entrepreneurs. Knowing the language and main concepts of accounting is a big help, not just for building credibility with VCs but also for running a successful business.

The next chapter continues the finance theme by looking at a company's business model. There are many options to consider.

The Business Model

There seems to be some perverse human characteristic that likes to make easy things difficult.

—Warren Buffett

In Mark Zuckerberg's letter to shareholders in February 2012, he made a brazen statement: "Facebook was not originally founded to be a company. We've always cared primarily about our social mission, the services we're building and the people who use them."

This is something you never hear from a public company's CEO. They would be fired! Even Google—which considers itself to be unconventional—doesn't have the same approach as Facebook.

According to Zuckerberg, "Simply put: we don't build services to make money; we make money to build better services."

Now that is unconventional. And it has worked extremely well. As you saw in the last chapter, Facebook has posted standout financials over the years.

For Zuckerberg, building social apps means avoiding the typical money-making aggressiveness that is prevalent in corporate America. Keep in mind that he could have easily plastered ads across Facebook, generating huge revenues. But Zuckerberg realized that this is the worst thing to do when creating an enduring company.

Just look at MySpace. From its origins, the company focused on monetizing—which became even more intense when News Corp. purchased the business. But it ultimately damaged the user experience and killed the company.

This chapter looks at strategies for pursuing a business model. You will first see how Facebook has done this and then examine other approaches that have proven to be successful as well.

Facebook's Business Model

The *business model* is how a company generates its revenues. When Facebook launched in 2004, the original vision was that it would focus on local ads. This made a lot of sense because the company was only in campus markets. As should be no surprise, there was a lot of demand for ads for local pizza joints and other cool hangouts. Classified ads were also popular because students moved frequently.

But as Facebook became ubiquitous, the business model evolved. As of now, it consists of two main sources of revenues: advertising and transaction fees from the Payments business.

Let's first look at the advertising business, which is the main source of revenue (about 80% in 2011). Facebook has two main approaches. One is to use a direct sales force to sell to major companies and ad agencies. These engagements can take time to close and often require developing sophisticated campaigns.

Facebook also has a self-service ad platform, which allows any advertiser to use an online system to manage their own campaign. This is mostly for smaller companies that don't have the budgets to hire advertising agencies.

Over the years, Facebook has invested heavily in developing systems for advertisers to get value from their advertising. The goal has been to demonstrate that there is a tangible return on investment (ROI).

Despite this effort, there have been concerns that social advertising is less effective than other approaches, such as Google-style search-engine marketing, television, and even radio. This was the conclusion of GM, which pulled all its Facebook advertising in May 2012. The belief was that the ROI was not compelling.

Perhaps one of the problems is that Facebook is a communications platform, which may not be optimal for serving ads because users are there to make comments, post status updates, and check out photos. Ads are often a distraction. It's true that Facebook has put them in unobtrusive areas—but this makes the ads even less effective because they are easy to ignore.

Another problem is privacy. It seems inevitable that there will be more restrictions on the handling of user information, which is used for targeting for advertising. The big question is how far governments will go.

But Facebook has continued to improve its advertising system. Some of these efforts include the following:

- *Targeting:* An advertiser can base ads on a group's demographics. Factors include age, location, gender, relationship status, educational history, workplace, and interests.

- *Social context:* Advertisers can engage a user's friends based on activities such as Liking the advertiser's Facebook page. The idea is that people probably value a friend's recommendations versus a straight ad.

- *Sponsored stories:* An advertiser can broadcast messages to more of its fans.

- *Analytics:* These track the performance of a campaign in real-time.

Although much of Facebook's advertising revenue has come from the web site, this started to change rapidly in 2012. There was a major shift to mobile traffic, which caught Facebook off guard. It didn't have the right infrastructure to monetize things, which resulted in a slowing of revenue growth. Traffic up, revenue down!

This was not the kind of message investors wanted to hear during the IPO in May and was a key reason for the lackluster reception. The good news is that Zuckerberg has declared mobile to be the company's number-one priority.

But solving the problem will take time. Mobile advertising is still in the nascent stages, and advertisers are experimenting with approaches, trying to see which get the most ROI.

This is why entrepreneurs need to be temperate about a business model based on mobile traffic. It could take a few years to generate any meaningful revenue.

The other important takeaway is that any type of advertising business model requires lots of effort. You need to hire top people, including those who can create campaigns as well as salespeople who can land clients. You also need to build an infrastructure that effectively delivers and measures ad impressions. Such things are not cheap and should be a big part of any venture funding.

Payments Business

The Payments system allows Facebook partners to charge for their apps. It involves the secure processing of credit cards, PayPal transactions, gift cards, and other payment methods. Facebook gets a juicy 30% fee for all transactions.

In July 2011, Facebook began requiring that all social game operators use the Payments system, which resulted in a spike in revenues. The move was controversial with developers, but they understood the value of the platform.

Zynga accounts for much of the Payments revenues so far. But over time, this should change. Keep in mind that Facebook will likely get into other lucrative areas, such as allowing people to use their smartphones as wallets.

The temptation for entrepreneurs is to build their own payments system because doing so means more control over the process and improved customization of the user experience. But this approach is most likely to be a bad move. Payment systems are extremely expensive to create, requiring complex algorithms and security protocols. For most startups, the best approach is to outsource the function to a standout company like PayPal.

Revenue Drivers

Back in early 2003, Mark Pincus started one of the first social networks, tribe. net. It got lots of traffic but was extremely difficult to monetize because it catered mostly to people with alternative lifestyles. Pincus experimented with different approaches, such as charging premium subscriptions, but nothing worked. He eventually sold the company to Cisco.

When it came to Pincus's next venture, Zynga, he wanted to prove out the business model as soon as possible. He wondered if people would pay for digital items to advance to higher levels in a game. After a few tests, it was clear that some users definitely would do so, and this testing gave Pincus enough confidence to pursue his innovative business model.

But to make it a success, he needed to understand the main drivers. These became his laser focus.

With more experimentation and testing, Pincus realized that there were some key factors. Perhaps the most important was daily active users (DAUs). Growth in this metric had the highest correlation to revenue generation (this has also been the case with Facebook). Pincus focused heavily on finding ways to boost DAUs, such as aggressive advertising. He once said in a media interview that when he sees a person, he thinks of them as a DAU!

Pincus' two-step process—to test the business model and find the drivers—is critical for any entrepreneur. Using a random approach is destined for failure, as seen with tribe.net.

Business Model Innovation

From time to time, a company creates a game-changing business model. This was certainly the case with Google AdWords.

But it took several iterations to get it right. Google AdWords started as a simple way to buy text-based ads related to search results. They were separated from other search results and clearly described as advertisements. This allowed for a more authentic user experience.

AdWords did generate lots of revenues and was profitable, but the system was no different from any other Internet company. Simply put, advertisers would bid on common search phrases and the highest bids would get the best rankings. Then, a couple of years later, Google added a crucial twist: the auctions didn't just rank ads on the amount of the bid but also factored in relevancy. The more clicks an ad got, the higher it was ranked. It was a huge breakthrough and resulted in explosive growth for Google: the ads were much more meaningful for users, which meant advertisers got high-quality leads.

But the company didn't stop there. Google broadened the business model by also introducing AdSense, which allowed third-party web sites to host AdWords and get a piece of the revenue. It helped propel the business to amazing heights. Competitors like Yahoo! and AOL could not catch up.

Facebook is trying to invent innovative business models as well—but it knows that doing so is extremely tough. To help, the company has engaged in a great deal of experimentation. For example, in New Zealand it's testing a new program called Highlight, which charges users to make posts to all their friends. It's still in the early stages but will certainly gauge a user's loyalty.

Business-model innovation may also come from acquisitions. Consider Facebook's purchased of Karma in May 2012. The company is an early player in the gift-giving mobile app business. The idea is that Facebook can leverage its social graph to make it easier to recommend gifts to friends, which may result in a massive market for social commerce.

As is the nature of experimentation, many things fail, and Facebook's experiments are no exception. Its Beacon advertising system, which was launched in 2007, was a total failure because people didn't want their friends to see their online purchases. There was also a failed attempt to replicate a Groupon-type business.

Nevertheless, it's worth the effort to be creative with your business model—and it should be an ongoing process. It can easily take a couple of years to refine the model.

But this is not to say that your business must innovate a business model. Many businesses do just fine using traditional approaches. The rest of the chapter looks at the primary ones.

Marketplace

This can be an extremely powerful business model. An example is eBay: it started as a way to sell Pez dispensers, but the platform proved versatile enough to sell virtually anything.

Even during the crazy dot-com era, eBay was one of the few companies that generated strong revenues and profits. The company didn't need any outside cash but raised venture capital anyway so as to attract a top-notch executive like Meg Whitman.

Why are marketplaces great businesses? A key reason is that they allow members to generate extra income. With eBay, there are people who make thousands of dollars per month; some have made it their full-time business.

Over the past decade, other marketplaces have emerged. One of the most notable is Airbnb. At first, the company began as a way to rent someone's couch to crash on! But the founders realized the business had much more potential: why not let people rent their apartments or homes to vacationers? It was a brilliant epiphany, and Airbnb turned into an instant hit, with huge revenues. The estimate is that the company will exceed $500 million in 2012.

Once a marketplace hits critical mass, it's tough to dislodge. After more than 16 years, eBay is still the biggest player in online auctions. And it looks like this will remain the case for many years to come.

But there is something that can derail a marketplace: loss of trust. If users feel they may get ripped off, it can be a disaster. In the early days of eBay, the company had to deal with members who sold items and didn't deliver them. As a result, the company took a variety of actions to reduce this activity. A key was implementing user ratings, which allowed for peer pressure.

Airbnb has had to deal with similar problems with user trust. In a couple of high-profile cases, members' homes were trashed and valuable property was stolen. Airbnb took actions to deal with the issues, such as offering video verification systems and a personal property guarantee (up to $1 million). There is also a 24-hour customer-support line.

Entrepreneurs looking to create a marketplace need a lot of realism. It's a proverbial chicken-and-egg dilemma: to get buyers, you need people to sell stuff; but to get sellers, you need buyers. The key for a successful marketplace is to continually find the right balance, which takes a tremendous amount of effort and good timing.

Freemium

A *freemium* means you have a fully functional free version of your product as well as a premium version. Because of this, it's easier to get new users. Who doesn't want to get a free product—especially one that provides a lot of value?

But the business model can be tricky. You need to have a low cost structure so you can make money from upgrades, which are based on a small number of users. The typical conversion rate is 1% to 5%. In other words, you need a large user base—say, over several million—for the freemium model to work. This has been the case with companies like LinkedIn, Evernote, Pandora, and Dropbox.

Once you have paid users, you need to make sure you provide strong ongoing support and innovation. If you don't, you will likely suffer from attrition, which can kill the freemium model.

In Silicon Valley, this business model is red hot, but many entrepreneurs set themselves up for failure. Many types of businesses don't have huge numbers of users, which means the freemium model probably won't reach critical mass.

Selling Data

Data can be extremely valuable and can be the basis of a compelling business model. It's been around for decades: companies like Dun & Bradstreet, Equifax, and Experian have made billions from the market. They have created extensive databases of customer information obtained from warranty cards, credit applications, magazine subscriptions, online forms, and so on.

But when it comes to using data from social applications, the level of skepticism is much higher. Perhaps it's because the medium is new or the information is deeply personal.

Whatever the reason, there has been considerable pushback about using the data-selling model when it comes to social apps. This is not to imply that there is no business opportunity. But it needs to be done with a lot of thought and clear-cut disclosure to users. Still, given the potential of online data, it could be the launch pad of a hugely successful business model over the next decade.

Commissions

Commissions have become a major source of revenues for Internet companies. This is especially the case for online travel companies, such as Expedia, Kayak, Priceline.com, and Hipmunk.

Commission revenues have two forms: *merchant revenue*, when the company charges the customer's credit card directly; and *agency revenues*, when the customer is referred to a third party and a commission is remitted. Which is better? Probably the merchant revenue approach, even though it's more expensive to implement. You have more control over the customer experience and should also be able to collect more information. In the end, it should result in higher revenues because a company has an easier time remarketing to its customer base.

Flawed Business Models

A company may show growth—such as in users—but not have a viable business model. An example is ICQ, which was one of the early players in instant messaging during the late 1990s. It quickly gained millions of users but was unable to generate much revenue. ICQ was essentially a feature, not a company.

When this is the case—and it's common—the best strategy is to sell out. Over the long haul, it will probably be quixotic to find a business model that works. In the case of ICQ, the company accepted a buyout from AOL. The huge Internet powerhouse liked the company because it gave users another reason to come back, which increased the opportunity to boost ad revenues.

On the other hand, a company's business model may generate lots of revenue but still have inherent danger. A typical scenario is when a company relies on major suppliers. This has been the case with Netflix. To build its highly popular video-streaming service, the company must invest huge sums in gaining access to premium content. The problem is that it has little negotiating leverage because it competes against mega-companies like Amazon.com and Comcast, which can pay even higher prices for content. Those competitors have the luxury of making up for the revenue shortfall by relying on their other businesses.

To avoid these kinds of business-model problems, you need to think about potential vulnerabilities. Is your product mostly a nice feature, or is it a stand-alone product? Might a larger competitor outbid you for content or distribution? Going through numerous scenarios is a very helpful activity and can help to avert disasters.

Finding the Ideal Business Model

When you're brainstorming and iterating your business model, there are some key things to keep in mind. Bill Gurley (a venture capitalist at Benchmark Capital, which has funded companies like Twitter, eBay and Instagram) wrote a blog about this topic and set forth some helpful factors.[1] Here's what he looks for:

- *Sustainable competitive advantage:* You need a way to deal with rivals for the long haul. It could be a great brand, network effects, or a strong infrastructure. Some companies have all three, such as Microsoft, Facebook, and Apple.

- *Predictable revenue:* Quarter after quarter, a company needs to increase its revenues. This should be not only because of a growing market but also due to strong pricing. At the same time, existing customers will continue to come back—and usually buy more of the company's product.

- *Customer retention:* This is a major factor for Facebook. Just imagine the hassle of reconstructing your social graph somewhere else!

- *Gross margin:* This needs to be over 70% or so. As you saw in Chapter 8, a high gross margin means much more latitude to invest in the product and marketing. It's also important that the gross margin tend to increase as revenues increase. This is a sign of a powerful business model.

- *Customer fragmentation:* A business model has risk if one or more customers represent over 10% of overall revenues. The reason is that they may have leverage in getting better terms. The ideal is to have a large customer base.

- *Marketing:* As much as possible, there should be small outlays for this expense item. Of course, Facebook had the advantage of being a highly viral platform that has been able to attract millions of users at extremely low costs.

---

[1] Bill Gurley, "All Revenue Is Not Created Equal: The Keys to the 10X Revenue Club," May 2011, http://abovethecrowd.com/2011/05/24/all-revenue-is-not-created-equal-the-keys-to-the-10x-revenue-club/.

Summary

This chapter has looked at how Facebook has evolved its business model and found highly effective ways to generate profitable revenues. You've also seen some other innovative approaches and considered some of the risks. It's important to remember that you probably won't figure out the right business model early on; it takes time to experiment. But a product generally has just one optimal business model.

The next chapter covers the often-mysterious topic of being a CEO. And yes, Zuckerberg has some extremely helpful lessons.

Being a Great CEO

Leadership and learning are indispensable to each other.

—John F. Kennedy

Have you heard of Jonathan Abrams? Unless you are tied into Silicon Valley, you probably haven't. Jonathan created Friendster in 2002; it was one of the first social networks. The site was an immediate hit and should have become the dominant player in the space, not Facebook.

Friendster raised substantial amounts of venture capital from tier-1 players like Kleiner Perkins Caufield & Byers, and Benchmark Capital. The company also received various juicy buyout offers, including one from Google.

Yet a couple of years later, Friendster imploded. There were many reasons— including destructive internal politics and too much focus on getting media attention—but a key problem was that the company had a feeble infrastructure. When millions of users hit the site, it slowed to a crawl. It often took over a minute for a page to appear!

Mark Zuckerberg learned some valuable lessons from Friendster, thanks to the fact that Peter Thiel, Reid Hoffman, and Sean Parker were Friendster investors. But avoiding mistakes was just one part of making Facebook great. Zuckerberg also needed to make strategic decisions about the product, business model, and funding. In other words, he needed to be a great CEO.

This chapter looks at some of the key takeaways from Zuckerberg's journey. The good news is that you don't have to be a natural-born leader to be a great CEO. It's definitely something that can be learned.

"CEO Lessons"

In the early days of Facebook, Zuckerberg was a terrible CEO. He didn't communicate well, he kept things to himself, and he often riled his employees. He also had a bit of an attitude. One famous example was his business card, which had the following at the top and bolded: "I'm the CEO, Bitch."

In late 2005, things were getting worse. Zuckerberg was spending most of his time hanging out with media moguls, flying private jets and dining at elite restaurants. These pastimes may have been a great ego boost, but they were taking a toll on Facebook's employees. Was the company up for sale? Would the owner be a global media conglomerate? Employees were becoming demoralized, and it was harming the company.

Trying to get things back on track, the company's in-house recruiter, Robin Reed, confronted Zuckerberg and said, "You'd better take CEO lessons, or this isn't going to work for you."

It was a pivotal moment—and a wakeup call. Zuckerberg was mature enough to evaluate the criticism and act on it. It was a valuable lesson and critical for the company's growth. From that point on, Zuckerberg set out to get CEO lessons from people who included some of the world's best leaders: Steve Jobs, Marc Andreessen, Jim Breyer, Bill Gates, and even Warren Buffett.

But perhaps the most influential—at least during the critical early years—was Donald Graham, CEO of the *Washington Post*. The two had an instant rapport. Zuckerberg was impressed with Graham's long-term strategic ideas about building a company that thrives across generations. To soak up information, Zuckerberg followed him around the offices.

No doubt, being a CEO can be lonely. You can't say something like, "I have no idea what to do. Any suggestions?" To do that would be a killer. This is why it's important to find mentors, as Zuckerberg did—especially those who have several rungs more experience than you.

But a CEO also needs to encourage an open environment. Employees should feel free to say negative things. If they don't, it will be nearly impossible for the CEO to understand the company's problems, especially as it grows at hyperspeed. The very fact that Reed was able to criticize Zuckerberg was an encouraging sign that Facebook had a culture of openness; and this became an element of his *Hacker Way*.

Zuckerberg's mistakes in the early years provided him with another crucial lesson: the perils of corporate imprinting. This is a natural human behavior in which employees copy their leader. If the CEO wears a hoodie, guess what?

Everyone else will. If they take up smoking, get ready for many employees to do so as well. And if the CEO gets married, expect lots of wedding invitations.

It's almost comic, but it's very real. This is why a CEO needs to be constantly aware of their own actions. How will they be interpreted? Is the right example being set? What about the nuances?

These questions can be vitally important for young CEOs, who may be on the wild side. This became a problem in the formative stages of Facebook, when the corporate environment was more like a raucous college dorm.

Having fun is a good thing, but there are boundaries. When things go too far, a company can alienate its employees and even trigger lawsuits. It may also result in chaos, which can make it tough to get things done.

Zuckerberg began to see problems emerge, and he took swift action to bring more professionalism to Facebook. He definitely set an example when he pushed out Sean Parker, who was an unabashed partier.

Unfortunately, it seems as though many of today's startup CEOs are not taking this approach. One example has been Groupon's CEO and co-founder, Andrew Mason. Since his company came public in late 2011, the stock price has plunged. A big problem has been the issue with the accounting and the financial system.

In 2012, Mason began have town-hall meetings with his employees to focus on finding ways to make the company more professional. Yet at the first meeting, he was drinking beer—and he burped! It was funny, but it continued the organization's goofy tone. It was so over-the-top that the story landed on the front page of the *Wall Street Journal*. It was the kind of PR the company didn't need and investors didn't want to see.

Beyond focusing on creating an open environment where criticism is encouraged, and understanding the dangerous consequences of corporate imprinting, what are some other best practices for budding CEOs? The rest of this chapter looks at the key factors of Zuckerberg's journey to becoming a great CEO.

Just Say "No"

As your business gains traction, you will inevitably attract lots of interest from third parties. There will be requests for partnerships or even buyouts. Of course, many salespeople will try to sell you stuff.

All of them will be convincing and complimentary about your company, but don't get sucked in. Perhaps one of the most valuable traits of a successful

CEO is the ability to say "no." Otherwise you'll get sucked into too many trivial activities, which means not having enough time for the important things.

In some cases, you need to put a stop to certain projects because they show few signs of success. It's not easy to do, but the costs of continuing such endeavors will only stunt your company's growth.

Zuckerberg has nixed many projects, such as a social calendar and the Deals business, even though significant resources had already been invested. But it didn't matter, because the efforts were not getting much interest. As the saying goes, "Fail fast."

Speed

Competing against mega-companies is daunting, and it may seem impossible to prevail. But there is something a small company can do that a big company can't: move fast. Always keep this in mind. It's a key advantage.

As your company grows, it's easy to allow friction to seep in. A CEO may become cautious and start avoiding risks, which is a natural response. But according to Zuckerberg, a company needs to keep moving "fast and break things." If you aren't making mistakes, then that's when you know you aren't working fast enough.

It's true that you should continue to engage in vigorous debate and analysis when making decisions. But you need to do so with urgency.

Zuckerberg has taken a direct and quick approach to making decisions. This means clearly stating his positions, listening to others, and then taking clear-cut action. This approach can seem impersonal and harsh, but it's necessary for success.

Avoid the Evils of Politics

Politics are the enemy of innovation. If employees are more concerned about their own agendas—and career paths—then they are about the business—it will be tough for a company to grow for the long haul.

Although politics can never be eliminated, they can be managed. Consider that Zuckerberg has made this a focus of his Hacker Way, which declares

> Hackers believe that the best idea and implementation should always win—not the person who is best at lobbying for an idea or the person who manages the most people ... Code wins arguments.

This approach is worth considering for your own venture. It should help keep up your company's momentum and unleash innovation. But it's critical that the CEO frequently talk about the importance of focusing on results, which must become part of the company's DNA.

Data-Driven

Many CEOs delude themselves: they ignore information to the contrary and think their business is doing well. Even CEOs of public companies have been known to do this.

During boom times, it's possible to thrive with this approach. Just look at the dot-com era. Showing metrics such as surges in users was enough to raise huge amounts of capital. But when the VC market collapsed, many companies were wiped out. Only those that focused on sound business models—like eBay, Priceline, and Google—were able to survive the nuclear winter.

To be a great CEO, you need to constantly track data and understand the trends. Although the implications may not always be clear—at least in the short run—you'll be in tune with the reality of your company.

Question Assumptions

This is a big one. A CEO should not accept the conventional wisdom. It's often wrong!

Zuckerberg has always been good at asking his team "Why?"—especially those who say something can't be done. This approach has been effective in reaching deeper truths, which may point to great product ideas or innovative business models. For example, when he thought about having a photo-sharing concept, it seemed like a bad idea. Did the world need another way to share pictures? But Zuckerberg found a way to use Facebook's social graph to make his version a game changer.

He has also focused on getting to the essence of things. This means constantly striving for simplicity. Consider that some of Facebook's best features include basic concepts like friends, Likes, and events.

Don't Be a Fake CEO

This is something that Zynga's Mark Pincus talks about. A *fake CEO* is someone who believes that image is everything. Such a person thinks of themselves primarily as a hot celebrity, not a leader who is focused on customers and the product. A fake CEO would rather post on Twitter or opine on matters at conferences.

In the meantime, the company doesn't have a real leader—just someone self-absorbed. Keep in mind that your employees have strong BS meters and should be able to easily detect when a CEO is superficial.

This is not to say that you should avoid publicity. As Chapter 7 discussed, PR is a great way to help grow your company and to become a thought leader in the industry. But don't believe your own press clippings.

A CEO needs to have a balance as well. Pursing the business on a 24/7 basis can quickly lead to burnout. Zuckerberg has dealt with this by setting a personal challenge each year. To meet one such challenge, he vowed to learn Mandarin Chinese; another year, he only ate meat from animals that he killed!

Setting these kinds of challenges is great, and they don't necessarily have to be focused on your business. It's better if they're beyond it. Having an open mind can be a big help in promoting innovation and bringing new perspectives.

Follow Your Passion

Since he was an early teen, Zuckerberg had a passion for creating applications. When he built something, it was usually a product he wanted for himself. There are cases where a successful entrepreneur may not necessarily be passionate about their business, but this can be tough to maintain in the long term.

Passion is contagious. It attracts top employees. It gets customers excited. It attracts the interest of partners. All these factors create a virtuous cycle, which helps to create great companies.

Summary

As you've seen in this chapter, there are no solid rules for being a successful CEO. All great leaders—such as Jack Welch, Steve Jobs, and Jeff Bezos—have unique approaches. Zuckerberg has evolved his own, and it has worked extremely well. The same will be the case for your own journey. Don't necessarily copy from Zuckerberg: a better idea is to learn from his ideas and see how they fit with your vision.

The next chapter looks at an area in which being a great CEO is critical: building teams.

The Team

Be nice to nerds. Chances are you'll end up working for one.

—Bill Gates

From the early days, Mark Zuckerberg knew he needed to snag super-smart engineers, and he spent a good amount of time on recruiting. But he also knew that intelligence isn't everything. Zuckerberg wanted *all* employees to fit into the corporate culture, which emphasized collaboration, excellence, and moving fast.

Hiring is a core competency at Facebook, and headcount soared from 2,126 to 3,539 from 2009 to 2011. And that's not the end of the company's growth. Facebook's headquarters in Menlo Park, CA, is about 2.2 million square feet. On the wall is posted an interesting phrase: "This journey is 1% finished."

In this chapter, you also take a journey: to understand the nuanced process of recruiting talent. It's a critical part of success—and extremely hard to pull off. You can learn from some of the techniques that have helped Zuckerberg put together a world-class team.

Mistakes and Stages

Many of your hiring decisions will be mistakes. That's a fact. Get used to it.

Zuckerberg learned this lesson quickly when he brought on Eduardo Saverin as his co-founder. Saverin was supposed to provide the business savvy for the company, doing things like creating the ad business and raising capital. But his efforts turned out to be underwhelming and even a hindrance to Facebook's progress. The company wasn't his top priority—he didn't even leave Harvard in 2004 to go to Silicon Valley with the rest of the team. That was a big-time red flag.

Zuckerberg took swift action and forced out Saverin. It was messy and gut-wrenching, but it was the right move.

Zuckerberg still needed a strong business partner, and he found that person with Sean Parker. It's true that Parker was wild and something of a party boy. For example, he hired graffiti artists to paint Facebook's offices (including risqué images in the men's bathroom).

Despite this, Parker proved to be invaluable during the company's initial success. He set up a Delaware C-Corp and put in place the mechanisms to give control to Zuckerberg (provisions in the shareholder agreement gave Zuckerberg the power of choosing the board members). Parker also made some key hires, including Matt Cohler, Kevin Colleran, and Aaron Sittig. He also helped with funding: he made key introductions to Reid Hoffman, Mark Pincus, and Peter Thiel.

But after a while, Parker turned into a liability. He was accused of questionable personal behavior, so Zuckerberg had to move him out. (Parker went on to help start companies like Spotify and become a billionaire from his stock in Facebook.)

Zuckerberg wanted some "adult supervision" to make sure Facebook would continue to grow. In September 2005, he hired Owen Van Natta, a former executive at Amazon.com. When he came on board, Facebook had only 26 employees and about $1 million in revenue. But Van Natta knew how to scale the organization and wasted little time in adding hundreds of employees. He also created the crucial infrastructure to accommodate the explosive growth, particularly in the sales organization and finance department. After a couple of years, Facebook reached $150 million in revenues. It certainly helped that Van Natta was a great dealmaker and negotiator.

In the meantime, Zuckerberg focused on the product, with the help of standout people like his school buddies Dustin Moskovitz and Adam D'Angelo. They were a tremendous source of energy and innovation, which helped to fend off rivals like MySpace.

By early 2008, problems were emerging. The launch of Beacon was a total disaster and hurt the company's credibility. Zuckerberg had no choice but to pull the product. Going forward, he knew he needed someone who could get the company to billion-dollar revenue levels. But Van Natta was the wrong person—his skill set was for early-stage ventures.

Zuckerberg went on another search and found Sheryl Sandberg. Even though she was only in her late 30s, she already had a stellar career. After earning an MBA at Harvard, she went on to be chief of staff of the US Treasury Department. In 2001, she joined Google; she eventually became vice president of global online sales and operations, where she helped to build the company's incredible business model.

Zuckerberg saw that Sandberg would be the perfect fit. But it wasn't easy bringing her on board. He spent several months wooing her with dinners, meetings at conferences, and lots of phone calls.

In March 2008, Sandberg agreed take the post of chief operating officer for Facebook, which was the number-two spot at the company. It turned out to be a great move. Within four years, Facebook hit $4 billion in revenues and $1 billion in profits.

It's important to understand that it's incredibly hard to find someone with the skill sets to scale a business to the levels Facebook has reached. It took about six years for Facebook to reach $1 billion in revenues.

Managing this growth is extremely difficult. What is it like to hire 500 employees in a year? More important, how do you manage them all? To be successful, you need a company with a strong organization, with people who can work at breakneck speed. The employees need to understand how to deal with the biggest problems. There is simply no time to waste on trivial issues—it will only slow the company's growth.

It's true that big-time risks are associated with hyper-growth. But when you're approaching a new market—such as social networking, social gaming, or daily deals—it's a race to get to dominance. Once that's achieved, it becomes tremendously difficult for others to threaten the market.

As you can see, building a team and scaling for growth is an evolving process. A CEO needs to realize that certain people may be best for only part of a company's life cycle. This means a new person will need to come on board to take the venture to the next level. This process requires a lot of strategic vision, but it's essential when creating a breakout company.

Before diving into the best practices of recruiting, let's first look at the topic of bringing on a co-founder.

Need a Co-Founder?

There's no easy answer to this question. It's true that many great companies have had co-founders, including Google, Yahoo!, Apple, and Microsoft. But other great companies haven't, such as Amazon.com and Dell.

There are certainly advantages to having a co-founder. You have someone to bounce ideas off, and you can benefit from the extra help (the work of a startup is enormous).

VCs will be encouraged because they will see your focus on teamwork, which helps minimize risks. But they also want to see co-founders with complementary skills. Often this means that at least one person has a technical background. At Facebook, Zuckerberg filled this role, but Dustin Moskovitz provided critical help with operations and the business strategy.

You need to be extra careful when finding a co-founder. Keep in mind that breakups are common, which can prove to be fatal. Ideally, you want a co-founder you've known for several years and with whom you have chemistry. They should also share your values and outlook on life.

Once you have the right co-founders, it's time to put together your core team. Let's look at some strategies.

Recruiting

Over time, you'll come up with your own style of recruiting. You'll learn from your co-founders and advisors, and you'll develop your own techniques. But to get things going, here are some ideas to consider:

- *Big-resume people:* When you grow, you need these types of employees. But when you hire them, put them at a level below what their skill set can handle. This is a good way to test the person and see if they truly believe in teamwork.

- *Walks:* Zuckerberg got this technique from Steve Jobs. He took long walks with potential recruits, which was an effective way to get to know the person and see if they fit with the corporate culture. Zuckerberg would often walk to the edge of a hill and say to the recruit that Facebook's best days were still ahead of it.

- *HR department:* Zuckerberg didn't believe that an HR person should be in charge. He hired a top engineer to run the department.

- *Interviews:* Resumes mean little. They don't give you any insight into key things like resourcefulness, ethics, and the ability to communicate. But an interview helps. It's good to include many people in the interview process: five to ten from across the organization. This may seem like a lot, but it's worth the effort. The costs of hiring the wrong person are much higher.

- *Hypothetical:* A good way to get a sense of a potential employee is to ask a question in the following format: "What would you do if …?" The answer should give you a good idea of the person's approach to decision-making.

- *Experience:* It's often not important. If anything, deep experience may mean that a person is set in their ways.

- *Work environment:* Create an environment that you would want to work in. When your employees see that your company is a great place to work, they will tell their friends. Some of the best recruits come from referrals.

- *Reviews:* The first six months are critical for a new employee, which is why you should have monthly reviews. But they shouldn't be just rundowns of employee progress. Employees should be empowered to provide their own feedback; and criticisms should be encouraged, not penalized. This is the best way to grow and to correct lingering problems.

- *Onboarding:* This sounds very corporate—and it is. But that doesn't mean it's a bad idea. From the start, you want to get your new recruits on the right track, which means providing intensive training. Facebook has a program called Bootcamp that all new engineers are required to attend. It involves courses on how to code the Facebook way.

Even if you wind up making a good hire, you must realize that the person probably won't be around for the long haul. Keeping top talent is never easy, especially when a person has so many opportunities.

Although it can be disruptive to have a key person leave your company, it should ultimately be healthy. Having new people come into the organization brings in new perspectives and skills, if only for a little while. This has been common for Facebook. One example was the hiring of Steve Chen, who only lasted a couple weeks; he then went on to co-found YouTube.

As you begin your entrepreneurial journey, you'll see that there are many ways to recruit—and it can be overwhelming. It's a good idea to test new approaches, but stick to a few that have a tendency to work the best for you. Otherwise the hiring process can become cumbersome, especially for the candidates.

You also need to refine your recruiting process for the roles you want to hire. Some of the trickiest include engineers and salespeople. Let's look at each.

Hiring Uber Engineers

It's easy to find uber engineers. The hard part is convincing them to join your firm.

Even a few uber engineers can make a huge difference for a startup. Their productivity levels are quantum leaps above those of good programmers.

This is why Zuckerberg spent so much time trying to get talented people like Adam D'Angelo, who was a graduate of the California Institute of Technology in computer science. While attending, he entered the Association for Computing Machinery International Collegiate Programming Contest, where he won the top spot in 2003 and second place in 2004. Zuckerberg believes that D'Angelo is the best programmer he has ever met.

While at Facebook, D'Angelo was critical in providing the underlying technologies to scale the company's tremendous growth. In a way, he helped avoid the kind of implosion that crushed Friendster.

How do you convince uber engineers to come on board? You need a compelling story. Zuckerberg had the advantage of Facebook's success, but he also had a grand vision. When he talked to people like D'Angelo, he told them they could have a huge impact on the world.

When recruiting uber engineers, you are competing against great companies like Google, Microsoft, and Zynga. You can't win by offering more money— you can't compete on this level. Success is a matter of getting an uber engineer excited about your company. It's that simple.

A good way at looking at this is via Abraham Maslow's hierarchy of needs. The most primal ones include food, air, and water. But as you move up the ladder, the needs become more ethereal. At the pinnacle, they include self-actualization and transcendence. This is where an uber engineer lives.

Another way to get the attention of an uber engineer is to show them the disadvantages of working for a larger organization. For the most part, the work won't be as impactful as it will be with a startup, and the person will probably occupy a cubicle.

As the CEO, you also need to convince the uber engineer that you will provide the support and tools necessary for success. This means investing in software, training, and other resources.

Despite all this, you should not hire an uber engineer at all costs. The person must believe in your mission and be willing to be a team player. It's far from easy to get a sense of this during interviews, but you can use some techniques to help:

- Avoid an uber engineer who talks mostly about compensation and exits. You instead want them to focus on ideas, the industry, and building great products.

- When discussing compensation, is it primarily about cash? If so, this is a bad sign. You want someone who wants stock.

- Can the engineer communicate complex ideas? To be successful, they will need to work well with others, and this means having strong communications skills.

- If your gut is unsure, this is a telling sign. Trust your instincts. You are probably talking to someone who won't work out.

As you begin hiring engineers, it's a good idea to form small teams. This is often best for increasing productivity and avoiding complexity. Consider Jeff Bezos's "Two Pizza Rule," which declares that an engineering team should be no larger than the number of people who can be fed with two pizzas!

Sales People

It's a myth that if you build a great product, customers will come. This is not the case even with Facebook. Over the years, the company has invested substantial amounts in building a global sales force.

Keep in mind that big brands like Coca-Cola and Proctor & Gamble aren't easily convinced to use a new ad system, even if it's from a well-known company like Facebook. They want to see results. They also want to get help when putting together effective ad campaigns.

Building a sales organization takes someone with lots of experience. It also takes several years to get momentum, because it's tough to find good sales people. Just like uber engineers, there aren't many around, and they prefer to work for larger organizations where the compensation is often much more lucrative. As a CEO, you will have to do some wooing to get top sales people interested in your company.

You also need a way to weed out lackluster sales people. One interesting approach is to ask for a person's W-2. Sales people are often the top-paid employees in an organization, so if a sales candidate is not willing to show their W-2, move on. They should be proud to show it!

In terms of running a sales organization, here are some techniques that can help improve results:

- *Constant analysis:* There's a lot of talk about *meritocracy* in Silicon Valley, and this is absolutely the case with sales people. Success can be measured, so there is nowhere to hide. Either sales people are meeting their goals or they aren't. And if they aren't, there shouldn't be much leeway.

- *Teams:* This concept is often alien to sales people. Sales is a Darwinian environment. But this can be harmful for the overall success of the company because it can hurt the customer experience. At Facebook, the company is known for making all best practices and learnings available to everyone—including the sales people.

- *CEO's role:* It's important for the CEO to make sales calls. It helps improve the performance of the sales organization and also shows that they care about its success. Another benefit: the CEO gets a better view of the company's customers.

- *The money machine:* This happens when the sales team begins to gel. You'll notice it when your company's revenues become more profitable as volume increases. At this point, you know you're reaching critical mass.

- *Quality:* A sale is only the first part of the process and means little. The real sign of success is when a customer is delighted. In this case, you benefit from ongoing business and should get referrals. Ideally, your customers will ultimately become rabid fans.

When it comes to compensation, a sales person gets a package that heavily emphasizes commissions. But a lot of thought needs to go into the scales, and this requires someone who has expertise.

You must also take a broader look at other forms of compensation, such as salary and equity. Of course, this is the case with any employee, even the office assistants.

Let's examine some good approaches when thinking about compensation.

Compensation Strategies

For a tech company, try to minimize salaries. You want to keep as much cash as possible available for investing in areas like infrastructure, marketing, and sales. Compensation should instead focus on the equity upside, which means shelling out less cash and also motivates employees to work harder. It's usually better when they think like owners, not hired help.

The most common type of equity incentive is the stock option, which gives an employee the right to buy a fixed number of shares at a certain stock price. In the early years, the stock price is often below $1. But if the company grows, the stock price is likely to grow substantially, creating strong gains for employees. In the case of Facebook, about a third of the employees were millionaires by the time of the IPO, thanks to equity compensation.

The exercise price of an option should be at or above the current fair market value (FMV) of the stock price. If it isn't, the IRS says the employee has received income and that a tax payment must be made. This also has adverse tax consequences for the company. So, it's important to get expert tax advice when issuing equity compensation. There should also be annual valuations, especially after the first major funding.

An option has a *vesting schedule*, which means an employee needs to stay with the firm for a period of time to earn the right to buy the shares. The most common approach is a four-year vesting period with a one-year cliff. To understand this, let's consider an example. Suppose you grant 80,000 shares to a new employee. They have to work for the company for one year to vest a quarter of the shares: 20,000. After this, a portion is vested each month until the end of the four-year period.

Over the past few years, some tech companies have been issuing *restricted stock* as well. This is a transfer of stock to an employee that isn't earned until the shares vest. When this happens, there will likely be a tax hit. Again, make sure you get help from a tax pro before making these types of decisions.

Outsourcing

Outsourcing can be a good strategy, but be careful. If you need work done on a core function, you probably should hire a person. A freelancer will not have the same kind of commitment or passion.

For the most part, freelancers are useful for short engagements or projects. But don't select one based only on a low rate; many freelancers are terrible and a huge waste of money. Before making a hiring decision, be sure you get referrals.

Another good way to get quality freelancers is to use sites like oDesk and Elance, which provide ratings for each service provider. They even give exams and tests for freelancers' skills and abilities.

In some cases, you may want to try *crowdsourcing*. This means you leverage a user base to develop something.

A variety of sites can help with this, such as 99designs. You post a project, and service providers submit mockups, such as for graphic designs. You then reward the best one with a bounty. Crowdsourcing can be a low-cost way to get quality results.

Facebook has also used crowdsourcing: for example, to translate Facebook into other languages. The cost of doing this using employees would have been prohibitive. Instead, Facebook created a platform that allowed its users to translate the content. It turned out to be a tremendous success.

Layoffs

Layoffs are brutal, but they are a natural part of the capitalist system. A decade ago, the dot-com industry went from a growth industry to a disaster. Layoffs were large and swift. In many cases they did little to help, because companies went bust anyway.

A CEO needs to be attuned to major economic downturns and big shifts in a market. The silver lining is that you can take advantage of a prior boom by diversifying your customer base and building a profitable business. This should help the company to survive. Interestingly enough, the economic downturn may be an opportunity, because you have less competition.

But dealing with the situation is critical. You can't live in denial. If you see clear signs of a major shift in the market or economy, you need to take quick action. As much as possible, make sure the layoffs are a one-time event. You don't want them to drag out over time, which will take a toll on morale and may wind-up destroying the company.

Let's hope you don't have to deal with something like this. If your company is successful, you will most likely be hiring lots of people.

Summary

As described in this chapter, you can use many approaches for recruiting success. The key is to experiment and hone those that work for you.

The next chapter looks at how to buy a company. It's been a highly effective strategy for Facebook and critical for getting top-notch talent.

M&A

Business opportunities are like buses, there's always another one coming.

—Richard Branson

In July 2007, Mark Zuckerberg made his first acquisition. It was a deal for Parakey, which was a startup based in Mountain View, CA. The company was developing technology to make applications work while online or offline, but this didn't matter to Zuckerberg. He wanted the company because of its talented co-founders, Blake Ross and Joe Hewitt. This type of deal became known as an *acqui-hire*.

Since then, Zuckerberg has gone on to strike over 25 transactions; the deal-making has accelerated over the past couple of years. All were acquire-hires but one: the $1 billion purchase of Instagram, which was a hugely popular mobile photo sharing site. Zuckerberg said the following:

> *This is an important milestone for Facebook because it's the first time we've ever acquired a product and company with so many users. We don't plan on doing many more of these, if any at all. But providing the best photo sharing experience is one reason why so many people love Facebook and we knew it would be worth bringing these two companies together.*

A key to acquisitions is having a clear thesis. Zuckerberg has certainly done this with his deal-making.

It's important because the failure rate of acquisitions is generally high. There are many risks, especially with integration. This chapter looks at some strategies to improve the odds.

Reasons to Buy a Company

It's easy to get *deal fever*: you become convinced that a deal is a must-have and that you should pay any price for it. But this approach often leads to disastrous results.

Before pulling the trigger on a deal, you need to be disciplined and have a solid rationale regarding the benefits. Let's look at some of the key ones.

Technology

Some companies are good at creating technologies but don't have the core team to commercialize them. It's a common problem.

The good news is that it can be a great opportunity for an acquisition. Keep in mind that a strong technology doesn't necessarily have a high value. It gets a premium only if it has traction with customers. A company like Facebook has the advantage of a huge user base and can often get immediate benefits from a new technology.

Another key technology asset is a company's patent portfolio. As has become apparent over the last few years, patent portfolios are extremely valuable, especially in categories like mobile and social networking. It's important to have an outside expert put a reasonable value on the intellectual property.

You may not necessarily need to purchase a company—a better approach may be to buy the patents directly. This is what Facebook did with Friendster in May 2010: it used 3.6 million shares to buy some of Friendster's social-networking patents.

Acqui-hires

As you've seen, sometimes a deal is about getting top-notch engineers, not a product or technology. But an acqui-hire is not easy to put a valuation on. For the most part, it involves getting a sense of the value of the numerous kinds of engineers in the marketplace, which can range from $150,000 to $1 million. The purchase price is mostly be in the form of equity, such as options and restricted stock grants.

But there must be more than a nice payday. The buyer must make a convincing case that their company offers greater opportunity. (Chapter 11 talked a lot about this.)

It's also critical that the CEO get involved in the pitch, regardless of the size of the deal. Zuckerberg is a big believer in this approach and has spent considerable time wooing founders.

User Base

An acquisition can be a quick way to get a footprint in a critical market. Google is one of the best at this. Deals for companies like Android and YouTube have been critical for the company's success.

But there are risks. A user-base acquisition often involves a high price tag. This is inevitable if the company has become the category killer and is growing at hyperspeed.

Reasons Not to Buy a Company

The problem is, the buyer may wind up stifling growth. Cultural disagreements can be immediate issues and result in key people leaving.

Sometimes the best deals are the ones you pass on. This is probably what Zynga's Mark Pincus thinks about his $180 million purchase of OMGPOP. When he struck the deal in March 2012, the company's Draw Something mobile game reached 14.6 million daily active users (DAUs). But within a few months, it plunged to 3.4 million.

The acquisition may still wind up being helpful. OMGPOP should provide Zynga with lots of expertise in the mobile market. But the goal of buying a user base has a good chance of being a failure.

Because of such risks, it's always a good idea to consider alternatives to an acquisition. One approach is to form a partnership, which may involve sharing technology or gaining access to a distribution channel. The partnership may provide the basis of an acquisition down the road.

Due Diligence

The letter of intent (LOI) is the first offer to purchase a company. It's a few pages long and sets out the main terms of the transaction, such as the valuation, retention bonuses, and protections in the case of misrepresentations or fraud.

After the parties sign the LOI, the buyer then engages in the due-diligence process, which can last a month or two. It should be obvious that confidentiality is of utmost concern in all discussions and exchanges of documents between the buyer and seller. Any inadvertent disclosure of sensitive information to competitors could be greatly damaging.

A smart buyer has already done some level of due diligence even before a deal is struck. You can do so by studying the market and keeping tabs on the seller.

Before Facebook bought Instagram, Zuckerberg already knew a lot about the company and had discussed a potential transaction with his board. When the time came that Instagram was ready for a deal, he was able to act swiftly.

But much of the due diligence comes after the LOI is signed. It involves a combination of activities including meetings, phones calls, and e-mails. It's extremely important to have a single point person for all the information. This manager is responsible for collecting and codifying the various reports and documents. In the end, it will make the process much smoother.

In some cases, the buyer uncovers undisclosed information that is damaging. It may be a technology that the seller doesn't own, or an imminent lawsuit. Such things may not be deal killers, but they probably mean the purchase price needs to be renegotiated. It's also a time for the buyer to have a frank discussion with the founder, with the main question being "What else hasn't been disclosed?" The buyer needs to emphasize that a strong relationship is key to the success of the acquisition, and that means there should be complete transparency.

Integration

Buying a company is not difficult. It's the post-deal integration that causes problems and often is the key reason for failed deals. The merger was the courtship; now both sides must find ways to make the marriage work.

Too often, the buyer underestimates how long it will take to get the two companies to act as one. When you take ownership of a second company, you've essentially created a new organization. You have to manage two: your old one and this new entity.

It's nearly impossible to conduct an effective integration without thorough planning. With a well-formulated plan, you have benchmarks against which to gauge your progress.

But even having a sound plan is no guarantee that you will avoid serious problems. The bottom line is that integration is tricky and tough. Some of the process requires a knack for dealing with people and new technologies. It's not a skill that can be rapidly taught—it's learned by doing.

Here are some things to consider when embarking on integration:

- *Customer care:* Rivals may try to poach customers. Often they use marketing campaigns to convince customers to move over. You need to make sure customers have a clear understanding of the acquisition.

- *Cost cutting:* Many tech acquisitions are about getting engineers, and there is a tendency to lay off the other employees. But this can be a blunder. The sales people may have strong relationships with customers, and the marketing people could have a good understanding of the target market.

- *Over-allocated resources:* Another big problem buyers run into is that they haven't factored in sufficient resources in terms of money and personnel time. It's smart to reserve additional money beyond what you've estimated.

The Integration Plan

Integration should be a joint effort, with representatives from both the buyer and seller (yes, integration is a team sport!). Try to involve the CEOs of both companies as well as some of the senior managers. Make sure the HR leaders participate actively as well. Much of the integration plan is about dealing with HR matters, especially layoffs and compensation.

Start the planning as early as possible, preferably when the LOI is signed. Developing a solid integration plan can take a month or so. And remember that the plan is not set in stone: it's a guide. If you realize that additional steps need to be taken, then do so.

An integration plan should cover compensation and benefits, organization integration, communications, and technology. For every category, establish a start date, a completion date, a list of people involved, and a desired outcome. To do this, you can use an online project-management tool like Zoho or Clarizen.com.

After the integration, you should have a post-mortem analysis. What were the problems? What worked? What lessons were learned along the way?

Compensation and Benefits

It's extremely rare for a buyer and seller to have the same compensation and benefit programs—in fact, it's virtually impossible. As a result, you need to spend quite a bit of time dealing with the differences. Pay, benefits, and stock options are matters of immense concern to employees, so this part of the integration needs to run smoothly. Even if the new employees don't like every modification of their old way (and they won't), it's critical that you present the overall package clearly and conclusively. And of course, if you want to avoid a stampede out the door, it's vital that the new deal be fairly equivalent to their old one.

Assuming you've conducted the due-diligence process thoroughly and systematically, you should have all the necessary documents to analyze the other side's compensation and benefit programs. You can then look at the features of both and make line-by-line comparisons. Doing so makes the process much more productive—and should help avoid major problems with employees.

Communications

Once the acquisition is announced, employees need swift communications. If this doesn't happen, expect rumors to spread. When an information void exists, it's filled—usually by false information. It's not uncommon for headhunters to try to poach employees when there is an acquisition.

When communicating with employees, here are some tips:

- *Announcement/FAQs:* You should send out e-mails and post information on the internal company web site. It can explain the deal and provide a timeline.

- *External communications:* Provide information to customers and vendors, too. Will the product change? Will it be kept? It's important to be clear-cut about the game plan for the acquisition.

- *Honesty:* If there is a question you can't answer, don't make something up. Instead, say you will get an answer promptly.

- *Layoffs:* Any layoffs should be done in personal meetings.

Summary

Expect lots of mistakes when acquiring a company. Even with a well-thought-out plan and a solid rationale, a deal may still be an abject failure. It's part of the nature of acquisitions. But Facebook has shown that such transactions are critical for building a successful company and are worth the risk.

The next chapter looks at the potential exit of your own company. This happens when you decide it's the best decision to sell out to a larger player.

Selling Your Company

The rich are different than you and me.

—F. Scott Fitzgerald

Yes, they have more money.

—Ernest Hemingway

It seems inconceivable that Mark Zuckerberg would ever sell his company. Keep in mind that he set in place powerful mechanisms to keep control. He has also rebuffed several mega-buyout offers.

Yet there was a point when Zuckerberg agreed to sell his company. It was in 2006, and he had a deal with Yahoo! for $1 billion. But then Yahoo! reported a weak quarter, and the stock price fell. The deal was off.

There is nothing wrong with selling your company. It's a much more likely outcome than going public. It can also be a stepping-stone to creating another company, which may turn out to be the real breakout opportunity. The first venture will certainly have been a great learning experience.

This chapter looks at the decision to sell out, describing the process and how you can make the right moves to maximize the outcome.

Deciding to Sell

There are many reasons to take a buyout offer. Some of the most pressing involve your company facing a rapidly competitive environment or a disruptive new technology. These forces can wipe out a company.

Just look at the case of Flip, which sold out to Cisco for $590 million in 2009. A few years before, the company launched a handheld camcorder that quickly dominated the market, with sales over 2 million units.

Cisco saw the deal as a way to break into the red-hot consumer market. But it turned out to be a disaster. The launch of Apple's iPhone disrupted the camcorder market, and Flip quickly flamed out. By April 2011, Cisco shut down the operation.

In the tech world, the time from success to failure can be painfully quick. So when you have a hot company, you need to do a gut check: is your product built to last? Do you have real, sustainable advantages? If not, then you should seriously look at selling out.

Other times, a company may sell out because the valuations have reached insane levels. A classic example is Mark Cuban. He was a natural born entrepreneur who started his first business when he was 12, selling garbage bags. He paid for his college tuition by collecting stamps and operating a pub he acquired.

In the early 1980s, Cuban saw the huge potential of the emerging PC market and launched MicroSolutions, a software reseller. He sold the company to CompuServe for $6 million.

But this was only a warm-up. In 1995, he co-founded Audionet with his partner, Todd Wagner, to broadcast Indiana University college basketball games. They soon realized that the opportunity was much larger, and they expanded their platform into many other categories. The company changed its name to Broadcast.com and went public. In 1999, Yahoo! bought the company for a whopping $5.9 billion. Broadcast.com had less than $20 million in revenue at the time.

Cuban was now a billionaire, but his wealth was in Yahoo! stock. Realizing that the dot-com boom could easily fizzle, he put a collar on his holdings. This was a sophisticated financial structure to give him downside protection if the stock plunged. It turned out to be a savvy move and meant that Cuban remained a billionaire. He went on to buy the Dallas Mavericks and fund other hot companies. His net worth is now about $2.3 billion.

Many other dot-com millionaires and billionaires were not so lucky. Many wound up with little, and some went bust. Chapter 15 looks at strategies for entrepreneurs to protect their hard-earned wealth.

Finding Buyers

When you decide to sell your company, you need to generate interest. The best scenario is to create an auction environment with multiple bidders, which should allow for a higher valuation. If your company is hot, you've probably already received buyout offers.

But how can you get more potential buyers to the table? One approach is to hire an investment bank, which provides a variety of services such as valuing your company and helping navigate the acquisition process. The firm also helps to identify the right types of buyers. This involves first putting together a pitch book that provides key details so as to elicit interest. The name of your company isn't disclosed, to maintain confidentiality. (It's never a good idea for the market to know that your company is up for sale; it may be seen as a sign of desperation.)

For its services, an investment bank gets an ongoing retainer and a percentage of the transaction. A common approach for arriving at the percentage is the Lehman Formula that goes back to the 1970s and got its start from the investment bank, Lehman Brothers.[1]

Amount	Fee
Up to $1 million	5%
2nd million	4%
3rd million	3%
4th million	2%
5th and beyond	1%

You should negotiate the fee, but don't be too aggressive. You want to make sure there is enough incentive for the investment bank to obtain a high price.

---

[1] www.investopedia.com/terms/l/lehmanformula.asp#axzz24ypDmf7P

Even if you don't use an investment bank, you should definitely get the help of an M&A attorney. It's also important to seek advice from your board of directors and other trusted advisors with experience in deal-making.

When you sell your company, there are no do-overs.

The Deal Process

The preliminary negotiations can take a long time. In some cases, a buyer may woo a candidate for several years until a deal is done.

But when a seller is serious, there is talk about the key terms, such as the valuation, the financial structure, and due diligence matters. These become part of the letter of intent (LOI), which is a nonbinding proposal to acquire the company.

The rest of this chapter examines the key terms in this document.

Price

This is often the main point of contention, as should be no surprise. In some cases, the price is easy to understand—for example, when the buyer offers an all-cash deal. But the seller may put restrictions on this. One way is with an *earnout*, which means the founder and employees receive additional cash or stock if certain milestones are hit.

The situation is much more complicated when the purchase price includes stock. This is especially the case when the buyer is privately held, because it's not easy to determine the stock's true value. If the seller doesn't go public or is sold to a larger player, you may wind up with little to show for the acquisition. This is fairly common.

It's often better to get stock in a public company, because the market is liquid. You can also check out the company's financial disclosures and gain a better sense of its performance.

But there are still risks. The stock you receive in an acquisition is *unregistered*, which means you can't immediately sell it. Until a company files a statement with the Securities and Exchange Commission, no sales are allowed for at least a year. A lot can happen during that time.

Regardless of the type of consideration, a transaction has various adjustment mechanisms that can impact the valuation. For example, a portion of the cash is held back in an escrow account (known as the *hold back*), to provide compensation for any breaches of the seller's promises. You can negotiate the hold back but not eliminate it. A typical approach is to have 10% to 20% of the purchase price set aside for about 12 to 18 months.

Another adjustment is for changes in the working capital. This accounts for any spikes in expenses or deterioration in the business that occur between the signing of the LOI and the closing of the transaction. It can be a substantial amount and weigh on the valuation. So, it's important for the seller to remain focused on the business's operations.

Money may also be put in escrow for *retention bonuses*. These are cash bonuses paid to management based on the time they remain at the company. During tech acquisitions, the buyer is often looking to keep talented engineers and managers for the long haul.

Deal Structures

There are generally two ways to structure an M&A deal: an asset purchase or a stock purchase.

Asset Purchase

An *asset purchase* means the seller transfers all or most of the assets of the business in exchange for stock or cash (or a combination of the two). This essentially involves a bill of sale for each asset, such as real estate, patents, trademarks, equipment and so on.

An asset purchase tends to be favorable for the buyer. Perhaps the biggest advantage is that there is no assumption of the company's liabilities, because they remain with the seller's corporation. But some jurisdictions still attempt to shift liability exposure to the buyer; this may be the case if there is evidence of fraud or product liability issues.

Another key to an asset purchase is that it provides tax benefits for the buyer. It allows for stepped-up basis in the assets purchased. After the acquisition, the buyer can depreciate the assets and get non-cash deductions, which should mean a lower tax bite.

An asset purchase may also result in terminations of contracts with suppliers. Keep in mind that contracts often contain *assignment clauses* that are triggered on an acquisition. In this case, the supplier may see an opportunity to renegotiate a higher price on the new contract.

Stock Purchase

If an asset purchase is not the right approach, then there is a *stock purchase*. In this case, the buyer purchases all or a majority of the shares from the seller. For larger transactions, the buyer may use a *statutory merger* (also known as a *reorganization*). It's based on state law—often in Delaware—that provides for potentially significant tax benefits.

The buyer assumes all the liabilities of the seller's company, which legally disappear. But the buyer may create a subsidiary and merge it into the seller's company. This is a smart way to help contain any potential exposures.

What if some of the shareholders don't want to sell out? A statutory merger usually requires only a majority vote, so all shareholders must ultimately tender their stock. There may be an appraisal right that lets a shareholder bring a court action to attempt to get a higher stock price.

Representations and Warranties

These are also known as *reps* and *warranties*. They are written expressions that document when a buyer or seller vouches for something, such as a company's finances, litigation, rights to intellectual property, and so on. For the most part, the reps and warranties are made by the seller. But if a company is selling to a private company, it's smart to get strong reps and warranties from the buyer, because it's more difficult to verify information.

A violation of reps and warranties during the negotiation of a merger can easily kill the deal or result in a lower valuation. If a violation occurs after the deal is struck, then damages may come out of the hold back. Or, if there is a carve-out, the buyer may have the right to go after the sellers personally. This can cause a hostile situation if they still work for the buyer. For this reason, it's important not to agree to any language that would result in personal liability for reps and warranties.

Negotiating reps and warranties is often a time-consuming and contentious process, because the buyer is taking a big risk in striking the deal. Might there be hidden time bombs? Does the business have major problems ahead?

To lessen the impact of reps and warranties, a seller has some options. They can use *materiality clauses*, which put a cap on liability exposure. For example, the reps and warranty for any lawsuits could state that there will be no liability over $1 million. Without this, the exposure could be unlimited.

Another helpful approach is the *knowledge qualification*. This means you agree to reps and warranties to the "best of your knowledge." It's a great way to minimize the liability exposure, because it's not easy for a buyer to prove what you knew at the time of the acquisition.

No-Shop Clause

This is standard. The buyer is making a substantial commitment and doesn't want to lose the deal to a rival—or have to pay a higher price. It's a reasonable position.

But you should negotiate the time period—which prevents you to seek out other potential buyers—anywhere from 30 to 60 days is good. This should be enough time to complete a deal.

Fees

Get the buyer to pay for everything, including legal fees and the investment banking fees, whether the deal goes through or not.

In rare cases, you may also get a *breakup fee*: a set amount that goes to the seller if the buyer terminates the deal. To help avoid this, the buyer will negotiate a *material adverse change clause*. This means the buyer can back out of the deal if there is a major deterioration in the business.

A breakup fee often ranges from 2% to 10% of the value of the deal. However, such arrangements are mostly for large deals, such as Instagram (the breakup fee was $200 million). These complex transactions can take six months to a year to complete; and there's always a possibility that antitrust authorities will block the deal. A breakup fee can compensate for the risks.

Employment Agreement

For tech deals, the buyer generally puts together employment agreements for key employees. When negotiating these documents, you should retain your own counsel; the corporate counsel looks out for the company's interests—not yours.

A major part of the negotiation is about compensation, so work hard to get a lucrative salary and equity package! But there are other critical areas to negotiate as well:

Termination

It's common for founders to be fired. They're going from being leaders to being employees, and it's a tough transition.

In the employment agreement, the buyer generally says it has the right to terminate employees for "cause." This statement seems innocuous, but it's fairly broad. You should limit it to areas like criminal activity, fraud, gross dishonesty, and consistent failure to discharge one's duties.

Even better, you should negotiate a requirement that there be "good reason" for termination. This makes the burden even tougher for the employer. Examples include materially changing compensation, depriving you of your title, or forcing you to relocate.

If you are terminated without cause, or there is no good reason, then you're entitled to some type of severance payment. This may include one to two years' worth of salary as well as full vesting of any options.

The severance payment may also be considered a *golden parachute* (if it's 2.99 times the average taxable income over the past five years). In this situation, you'll owe a 20% excise federal tax. Because of this, try to negotiate for a *gross up*, which effectively means the employer pays for the liability.

You should also ensure that there is no mitigation or offset clause. If not, then you may be required to give back part of your severance when you find a new gig.

Change of Control

If the buyer's company is also purchased, you should get full vesting of your options. In this scenario, there is a high risk that you will be terminated.

Insurance/Indemnification

If your firm is purchased by a public company, you may be considered an insider. This means you could be exposed to shareholder litigation. So, in the employment agreement, make sure the employer will cover you under the directors' and officers' policy and provide indemnification.

Noncompete Clause

Unless you are a rock-star employee, you need to accept this clause. The employer generally requires that—when you leave the company—you won't work for a rival or build a new company in the same space. The agreement should have a time limit, say one to two years. You also should try to narrow the industry focus in the clause.

Courts usually look unfavorably on noncompete agreements. The prevailing belief is that employees should have the right to work where they want.

But there is an exception: acquisitions. After all, part of the purchase price is exclusive use of the services of key employees. In other words, the noncompete agreements will likely be enforceable.

Summary

Selling your company can be stressful. Are you selling too soon? Might you be leaving lots of money on the table? Can you work as an employee with the new company? Before making a decision, you must think about your goals. You also need to negotiate hard, because there will be no way to undo the transaction.

The next chapter looks at another type of exit: an IPO. It can be a thrilling experience and create lots of wealth, but it has its own risks.

The IPO

You made a commitment to [our employees and investors] when you gave them equity that you'd work hard to make it worth a lot and make it liquid, and this IPO is fulfilling our commitment. As you become a public company, you're making a similar commitment to our new investors and you work just as hard to fulfill it.

—Mark Zuckerberg's letter to shareholders, February 2012

Ahead of the Facebook IPO on May 18, 2012, just about everyone around the world thought it would be a huge success. It seemed like a once-in-a-lifetime opportunity to make a killing. There were stories of people preparing to put their life savings into the stock.

To meet the demand, Facebook boosted the number of shares offered by 100 million and hiked the price range from $28–$35 to $34–$38. One report indicated that the offering was oversubscribed by 20X in Asia alone.

But on the day of the IPO, nothing seemed to go right. NASDAQ's computer system went haywire due to the influx of orders, and it took hours for investors to get confirmations. The stock went from $42 to $38.

But this wasn't the end of the deterioration. Within a few months, the stock dropped to $23, and investors lost $39 billion. The IPO dream turned into a nightmare.

The full story of the offering may never be known. But it offers some important lessons, which this chapter examines. Before doing this, let's cover the fundamentals of IPOs.

Reasons to Go Public

An IPO is when a company first issues stock to the public, usually through a national exchange like the NYSE or NASDAQ. There are many reasons to do this, but the primary one is to raise capital. Often, all the money goes to fund a company's growth. With larger companies, part of the proceeds may also go to buy the shares of insiders, including venture capitalists and employees.

Facebook raised $16 billion from its IPO, making it the second largest offering in US history. About 43% of the capital went to the company and the remainder to insiders. Here's a rundown:

Person	Cash-Out
Mark Zuckerberg	$1.15 billion
Peter Thiel	$640 million
Accel	$2.19 billion
DST Global	$1.74 billion
Goldman Sachs	$1.58 billion
T. Rowe Price	$229.3 million
Tiger Global Management	$74.4 million

Another important reason for an IPO is to gain credibility. A company must undergo rigorous auditing and compliance requirements first, so potential customers and partners have much more confidence in doing business with the company.

Being public also means a company can easily use its stock as currency to buy other companies. It has a discernible value and is liquid because it's traded every business day. The company also benefits from cash savings.

Once a company is public, it often becomes easier to raise additional capital. A group of investors understands the company's story and may be willing to buy more shares. It also helps that the company has been periodically publishing its financials.

When a company offers shares after an IPO, the financing is called a *secondary offering*. For the most part, a company does this when the valuation is fairly robust.

Disadvantages of Going Public

Facebook waited about eight years to go public. For a company of its scale, this was definitely a long time. Google, on the other hand, waited only about five years.

Zuckerberg made it clear that he wanted to wait as long as possible before becoming a public company. The primary reason he pulled the trigger on an IPO was an archaic federal securities rule, which said that once a company reaches 500 shareholders, it must begin making public disclosures through the Securities and Exchange Commission (SEC). The irony is that the rule was changed after Facebook began the IPO process; the new limit is now 2,000 shareholders.

Why did Zuckerberg have such an aversion to going public? One key motivation was his desire to keep private the company's plans and financials, which helped to give Facebook a competitive edge.

But perhaps the most important reason was that Zuckerberg didn't want the distractions of dealing with public shareholders, Wall Street analysts, and the onerous regulatory requirements. Most Wall Street investors—except a few like Warren Buffett—want to see short-term results and will dump a stock if it doesn't meet lofty expectations. When Facebook reported its first quarterly report, Zuckerberg got a striking example of this behavior: the stock plunged 12%. But he didn't let it change his long-term approach, which he emphasized on Facebook's first earnings conference call as a public company.

Because of the plunge in the stock price, Zuckerberg got first-hand experience with yet another negative aspect of IPOs: shareholder lawsuits. It didn't take long for lawyers to put together complaints and make him the defendant. Although Facebook has sufficient insurance and legal resources to fight the lawsuits, they are still a major distraction for the company.

A stock plunge can even encourage hostile takeovers, but Zuckerberg wisely implemented a structure to minimize this possibility. He created two types of stock: Class A and Class B. The Class B stock gave him 10 votes per share, and the Class A stock had only one vote. This meant Zuckerberg maintained nearly 56% of the voting power after the IPO, which would make it incredibly difficult for an outside shareholder to gain control. The dual-class structure has been popular with other major social media operators like Zynga, LinkedIn, and Groupon.

An IPO also means a company is saddled with ongoing costs that can easily range from $3 million to $5 million a year. These expenses are for lawyers, auditors, and investor relations firms. They are critical for putting together the financial disclosures and implementing the core systems to make sure the company is in compliance with the myriad laws and regulations.

At the core of all this is the Sarbanes-Oxley (SOX) law. Congress passed the landmark legislation in 2002 in response to the accounting scandals at Enron and WorldCom. The goal was to make corporate fraud a thing of the past.

It was certainly a good idea and helped to bring back confidence in the markets. But the requirements proved to be fairly onerous. For example, a company's CEO and CFO must sign the quarterly and annual reports. If these disclosures wind up being fraudulent, these executives may face fines of up to $5 million and prison terms of 20 years.

But perhaps the toughest requirement is Section 404, which requires that an auditor test a company's internal controls and financial system. This can be a time-consuming and expensive process.

SOX certainly helped to reduce corporate fraud, but it also meant far fewer IPOs. This definitely isn't a good thing, because a healthy financial market is critical for encouraging the creation of new ventures. Investors have a bigger incentive to put money to work if IPOs are a likely option.

In 2012, President Obama and Congress passed legislation to pare back SOX with the passage of the JOBS Act. It reduces some of the disclosure requirements and eliminates the need for Section 404 if a company fits the definition of an *emerging growth* company (has less than $1 billion in annual revenues). It's too early to tell what the impact of the JOBS Act will be. But by lessening some of the burdens from SOX, it should have a positive impact and allow for a more robust IPO market.

Getting IPO Ready

An IPO can take from 6 to 12 months. In addition, much preparation is required to get the company *IPO ready*, which involves implementing a strong financial reporting system and hiring key senior executives. Such efforts can easily take a year or more.

In the case of Facebook, a key hire was Sheryl Sandberg, who became the company's chief operating officer. Facebook also filled the critical role of the chief financial officer (CFO): this spot went to David A. Ebersman, who came on board in September 2009. Before this, he was the CFO of Genentech, a major biotech company. He also had Wall Street experience as a stock analyst at Oppenheimer & Co.

Besides a strong senior management team, a company also needs to retain top-notch advisors. The main ones are described next.

Underwriter

An underwriter is a Wall Street firm that manages the IPO process. Responsibilities include drafting the prospectus, coming up with a valuation, and locating the right investors.

An underwriter is generally compensated based on the amount raised, ranging from 2% to 7%. But Facebook's underwriter, Morgan Stanley, received only 1%, primarily because all the top underwriters worked aggressively to get the assignment due to its high profile.

Attorneys

Many attorneys are involved in an IPO. They help with the complex legal issues inherent in state and federal securities laws.

It's important to retain a firm that has significant experience with the process and also knows how to deal with the SEC. You may even need to hire overseas law firms, if the IPO has substantial interest from foreign investors. For example, Facebook issued large numbers of IPO shares to investors in Europe as well as Japan and Singapore.

Auditor

This is a firm that vouches for a company's financial statements. For an IPO, the auditor must be registered with the SEC.

The auditor performs a variety of duties, the most important of which is to issue a *comfort letter*. It provides assurance that the financial statements are in accordance with Generally Accepted Accounting Principles (GAAP).

In some cases, an auditor issues a *going concern* statement. This means it believes the company may be vulnerable to going bankrupt!

Becoming a Real Company

To get ready for an IPO, a company needs to do more than just get its books in order and hire top people. It also needs a highly disciplined approach to product development.

Zuckerberg has had to go through this evolution. In the early days, he provided no warnings about any changes to the Facebook platform—he just released the product or feature. This was jarring for users, and often, many complained. Zuckerberg considered it a positive sign because there was lots of passion about the product.

But as an organization grows, the seat-of-the-pants approach can be fatal. Zuckerberg has made some major changes in his strategy, which has become much more methodical. This was evident in the development of the Timeline. The project's origins go back to brainstorming sessions with Sam Lessin, a Harvard pal of Zuckerberg who came on board Facebook through the October 2010 acquisition of Drop.io.

Once he had some clear ideas, Zuckerberg set in motion a careful project plan that lasted 18 months. It involved the kinds of things you would have at any big company, such as focus groups and many iterations (there were more than 100 different versions of the Timeline).

To test the Timeline, Facebook first launched it on an experimental basis in New Zealand. This was an effective way to get valuable feedback and tweak the product. At the same time, Facebook began educating advertisers and development partners; they needed to be ready to make for a smooth transition.

This kind of discipline can be a hindrance to an early-stage company. But as time goes by, a transition is necessary. It can be tough and full of mistakes, but it's essential in order to scale growth.

The IPO Process

When a company decides to go public, it must first select a lead underwriter. The process is called a *bake-off*, and it involves numerous presentations. A company may hire two or more lead underwriters (called *co-underwriters* or *co-managers*); sometimes this is about showing more credibility. For tech companies, it's common to have Morgan Stanley and Goldman Sachs as co-managers.

Of course, a company wants other benefits in addition to brand value. For example, it's smart to see if an underwriter has strong retail investor bases, respected analysts, and an extensive trading organization. Post-IPO services are also important. A top underwriter provides advice on matters like mergers and secondary offerings.

Once a company selects an underwriter or co-underwriters, there is an all-hands meeting. This sets forth the main goals and timetable.

The first deliverable is the *prospectus*, also known as the *S-1*. It includes the financials, risk factors, executive compensation, financing history, and business plan. Until the S-1 is filed with the SEC, the company is not allowed to make any announcements about its intention to go public. Violating this rule is called *gun jumping* and can mean delaying the IPO.

An underwriter also has a *letter of intent* (LOI) with the company, setting forth compensation and other terms. It's not binding until a day before the IPO. At this point, the underwriter is required to write a check to the company even if it can't sell shares to the public.

After the S-1 is finished, the underwriter submits it to the SEC. After a month or so, the federal agency sends back questions to the company (known as *comments*). These can be contentious, as happened with Groupon. The company pushed back hard on several questions about its accounting. In the end, that turned out to be a big mistake, because the company had to restate its earnings for its first quarter as a public company. It was a huge embarrassment.

Facebook had a smooth process. It helped that the company took a conservative approach to its financials and accounting principles. This strategy is good for any company.

Selecting an Exchange

The choice of an exchange is usually between the NYSE and the NASDAQ. The tradition is for early-stage tech companies to list on the NASDAQ.

But this has been changing: the NYSE has snagged top listings from companies including Pandora and Yelp. The trend may accelerate as a result of the NASDAQ's botched IPO of Facebook.

There are some trading platforms you should avoid, including the OTC Bulletin Board and the Pink Sheets. These are mostly quotation services that provide much less oversight. The trading volume is usually thin as well.

The Road Show

During the *road show*, also called the *dog-and-pony show*, senior management spends one to two weeks making presentations to investors. For the most part, they are in major US cities like Los Angeles, Boston, New York, Dallas, and San Francisco. But in some cases, management may make presentations in Europe and Asia.

Facebook's road show mostly included Ebersman and Sandberg. Zuckerberg attended only two presentations, and he caused a media stir when he wore his hoodie and sandals.

During the road-show process, the lead underwriter gauges investor interest. This helps to establish the price range of the offering. If demand is strong, the underwriter may increase the price range as well as the number of shares.

If there are any changes to the prospectus during this period, the company files a *free-writing prospectus* (FWP on the SEC's web site). Facebook filed one on May 5, 2012; it disclosed some weakness in the business due to the rapid shift to mobile. The disclosure may have been a key factor in some of the loss of enthusiasm for the deal and was also an ominous sign that the first quarter report would be relatively weak. But Facebook had little choice about making the filing—the SEC always demands disclosures of material changes in the business.

IPO Day!

A couple of days before an IPO, the underwriters send an *acceleration request* to the SEC, which declares the S-1 to be *effective*. The company can now sell its shares to the public.

On the night before the day of the IPO, the underwriter and the company decide on the offering price. This can be a heated discussion. The company wants to raise as much money as possible. The underwriter, on the other hand, wants to make sure investors get an attractive return. Facebook's pricing meeting lasted only about 10 minutes because there was already a consensus on $38 being the best price for the IPO.

Once the price is set, the underwriter notifies investors and allocates shares to them (usually fewer than the number requested). The reason is that there is generally more demand than there are available shares.

On the day of the IPO, the CEO often rings the bell on the NYSE or opens the NASDAQ. There are also lots of media interviews. An IPO can be a great branding event.

Culture Change

If you're in your 20s and worth millions, will you be motivated to keep working hard? Perhaps not. This is a huge challenge for any highly successful company that comes public. Facebook's IPO created more than 1,000 millionaires.

The challenge for the company is to find ways to maintain the passion and enthusiasm. This is why Facebook had a hackathon on the night before the IPO. It was a strong reminder that the company needed to focus on the future.

But maintaining the hacker culture could be Facebook's biggest challenge. A concept called *vesting in peace* (VIP) describes a top employee who works just enough to not get fired and give up their options. This is common in Silicon Valley.

Another issue is the disparities in wealth. Recent employees don't share in the riches, but they see others buying big homes and nice cars. This can cause envy, which hurts productivity.

There are no easy ways to deal with these cultural issues. The key is for the CEO to be a strong leader and show that they're committed to the long term. So far, Zuckerberg has not backed off from this commitment.

Lessons of the Facebook IPO

A key takeaway from Facebook's public offering is the importance of getting the valuation right. It's a difficult topic, even for a well-established company like Facebook, primarily because the technology industry involves tremendous uncertainty. Once-towering companies like Sony and Yahoo! can eventually become laggards. Many disappear or are bought out.

Although Facebook went public with strong financials, there were still worries about the future business. For example, an executive provided lowered revenue and profit guidance to an analyst at Morgan Stanley. The analyst then lowered his own projection and told several major investors about it. There was nothing illegal about this, but it spooked investors.

At the heart of the analysis was the rapid shift from desktop traffic to mobile devices. This change seems like a good thing, but Facebook didn't anticipate it and failed to develop advertising systems to monetize its mobile apps.

At the same time, another piece of news created more uncertainty: GM planned to cut off all its advertising on Facebook. The company is number three in terms of ad spending in the US, so its drastic move was noteworthy.

Investors began to get skittish. Was Facebook's growth decelerating? When would it find the right business model for mobile? Was the GM problem just the beginning of more defections? In light of all this, it seems reasonable that the company should have been more tempered with its valuation.

It's important to realize that public markets have different kinds of investors. Many of them don't necessarily understand new-fangled technologies and try to avoid paying premium valuations for stocks. Facebook should have seen this poor performance in prior offerings, such as for Zynga, Pandora, and Groupon.

In addition, many top Wall Street investors still have fresh memories of the dot-com era. They don't want to get trapped in another bust that could tank their returns.

Facebook and Morgan Stanley apparently ignored these signs. They instead focused too much on the high valuations in the secondary markets, where Facebook's stock routinely traded in the low to mid 40s.

But the secondary markets are much less liquid than public markets, and the investors are different: many of them are deeply bullish on the prospects for tech. So it makes sense that they would pay premium prices for the shares.

Valuation was not the only problem. Zuckerberg was too lackadaisical about the IPO process. He got married a day after the offering! It was a brazen move and did little to encourage confidence from investors.

Going forward, Zuckerberg may change his approach. If he wants to have a thriving business, he needs to be mindful of Wall Street. Other standout companies have done this, including Microsoft, Google, and Apple. It does seem as though Zuckerberg has learned his lesson: an example was his active role on Facebook's first conference call with investors.

Summary

This chapter looked at the key steps of an IPO and ways to help improve your chances of success. Even though the regulations are less onerous than in the past, only top-notch companies can be successful in the public markets. Investors ignore companies that fail to show consistent growth, which means a poor stock price.

The next chapter examines wealth management. It's a topic that entrepreneurs may ignore, which can be a big mistake.

Wealth Management

I am not so much concerned with the return on capital as I am with the return of capital.

—Will Rogers

Mark Zuckerberg is the second youngest billionaire in the world, with the number-one spot going to his co-founder Dustin Moskovitz. (He's only eight days younger than Zuckerberg.)

But unlike other tech billionaires—such as Oracle's Larry Ellison and Microsoft's Bill Gates—Zuckerberg doesn't have multiple estates, yachts, and other nice toys. He lives in a $7 million home in Menlo Park, which seems kind of underwhelming for a billionaire. He had to get a loan from Moskovitz for the down payment!

Wealth doesn't seem overly important to Zuckerberg. When he had a chance to sell Facebook and walk away with a huge payday, he said no. He was on a grand mission to change the world, and this would not be possible if he sold out.

Zuckerberg is mindful of sound wealth management. During the IPO, he sold $1.15 billion of stock to handle the exercise of his stock options and pay his taxes. He also set aside millions to make sure he can pay his bills.

This chapter looks at the unique financial needs of entrepreneurs and how they evolve as a company grows. Some of the topics include secondary markets, core financial planning principles, asset protection, and philanthropy.

The Startup Days

Chances are, you'll have little money when you launch your venture. To keep afloat, you may even need to have a part-time job and live with a roommate.

A key trait for success is to live on an extremely low income. To help things along, it's a good idea to track every penny and use a service like Mint.com. It also helps to learn about some of the fundamentals of personal finance. The good news is that there are many great sites to help out, such as Money.com, Kiplinger.com, and BankRate.com.

Even when you raise capital, your salary will likely be modest, because investors want to make sure you are motivated by equity. Peter Thiel believes that a CEO should make no more than $150,000 a year. In many places this may seem like a lot, but definitely not in tech hotspots like Silicon Valley and New York.

Secondary Transactions

After several rounds of capital, your company may be worth over $100 million, and that means you are officially a multimillionaire. Although this is a big achievement—and kind of surreal—you have a problem: until you sell the company or go public, you can't turn much of this wealth into cash.

But there is a way to get some liquidity: through secondary markets. These are online platforms, such as SecondMarket and SharesPost, that let founders and employees sell some of their privately held shares.

It should be no surprise that Facebook was the most popular stock sold in the secondary markets from 2008 to 2011. The sales helped employees to diversify their wealth into other investments and to even fund their own startups.

But before you do a transaction, talk to your investors. They should understand your needs and realize that it's important to reap the rewards of your success. The investors may also be interested in buying the shares or know other value-add purchasers, which can keep the equity in friendly hands.

If you decide to use a secondary exchange, the process takes anywhere from 30 to 45 days. The first step involves getting numerous bidders, who should undergo background checks. Once a qualified buyer is located, there is some paperwork, such as drafting a purchase agreement; it's a good idea to have a qualified attorney review everything. The buyer sets aside money in an escrow account that won't be released until the stock certificates are sent to the buyer.

For the service, a secondary exchange usually charges a fee that represents a percentage of the transaction, such as 1% to 5%. But as with anything in business, you can negotiate this payment.

How much of your stake should you sell? There are no clear-cut rules. From a financial planning standpoint, it makes sense to sell at least two to three years' worth of your salary. It's common for founders to eventually leave a company due to burnout or to pursue another early-stage venture. If you have a considerable amount of money set aside, you aren't under pressure when you decide to make a big change in your career path.

Early-stage ventures are extremely risky—look at the case of Digg, which was a social media darling but could not keep up against rivals like Facebook. But the company's co-founder, Kevin Rose, was able to sell enough of his shares to pursue other ventures. He also had enough to invest in breakout companies like Twitter and Zynga.

If you have a chance to get some liquidity from your venture, it's probably best to do so.

The Big Time

Back in the late 1980s, John McAfee launched McAfee Associates and pioneered the fast-growing market for antivirus software. His distribution model was pathbreaking at the time: it involved giving away the product. If customers liked it, they paid for a subscription. McAfee Associates saw explosive growth, and the company went public in 1992.

This would have satisfied many entrepreneurs, but not McAfee. Bored with the corporate life, he left McAfee Associates a few years later and cashed out about $100 million. He went on to invest aggressively in real estate and tech stocks. He even put his money in high-yield bonds from Lehman Brothers!

McAfee's strategy worked well until the financial system nearly collapsed in 2008. In the aftermath, he had only about $4 million remaining.

This tale is common in the tech world. A key reason is that entrepreneurs love to take risks. This may be fine when you're creating a new venture, but it can be the worst approach when managing your personal finances. The global markets have seen considerable volatility over the past decade, including the popping of the dot-com and real-estate bubbles.

When looking at your personal finances, it's important to have a realistic and balanced approach. To help things along, here are some things to consider.

Risk vs. Reward

If you want the potential for high returns, then you need to take risks. This is a truism in investing. So if a financial advisor pitches you an opportunity that can generate large gains but says the risks are minimal, move on. It probably has tremendous risk!

Over the past few years, there has been a surge in big-time scams. The most notorious example is Bernie Madoff, who pulled of a $65 billion Ponzi scheme. Always remember: If it seems too good to be true, it is.

Core Portfolio

Mutual funds and exchange-traded funds (ETFs) offer tremendous advantages for building your wealth. They provide exposure to the main asset classes, such as stocks, bonds, and real estate. A rule of thumb is to have more than half of your liquid wealth in these types of investments.

How much should be in each category? It's a matter of your goals, family situation, and age. A reputable financial advisor can provide some helpful advice on asset allocation. There are also some great web services, such as Wealthfront, which is focused on the needs of tech entrepreneurs.

Safe Haven in Times of Panic

This usually means buying gold. I recommend that this asset make up 5% to 10% of your portfolio. The good news is that it's much easier to own gold— compared to five or six years ago when you had to find a place to store it— such as with the purchase of SPDR Gold Shares (GLD). It's an ETF that is backed by gold bullion, which is stored in vaults in London.

Gold has historically been a safe haven during times of distress. And if the future continues to see volatility, this precious metal should be a stabilizing force in a portfolio.

Alternative Investments

These are simply investments that are not stocks or bonds. They are diverse, including things like commodities, timber, and currencies.

One way to get exposure to alternative investments is through hedge funds. The money managers usually have wide latitude, such as the ability to engage in short selling. This makes it possible to make money when an investment falls!

But hedge funds have high fee structures. The money managers usually have a 2/20 approach: this means they get 2% of the assets under management and 20% of the profits generated.

There may even be *lock-ups*, in which an investor isn't allowed to sell their position for a couple of years. This can be agonizing during times like the 2008 financial crisis.

When selecting a hedge fund, make sure you do a lot of homework. Get referrals from existing investors, and do background checks on the money managers. A top financial advisor can also provide help.

Angel Investing

As you get rich from your startup, there's a good chance you will begin engaging in angel investing. It can be a lot of fun, but the risks are substantial. For the most part, these investments go bust. And even for those that are successful, the returns may not be realized until three to five years down the road. As a result, you should have a low percentage of your net worth in angel investments—probably less than 5%.

Taxes

This is a critically important factor. Saving 5% or 10% on taxes can be a big deal. Services like TurboTax are excellent, but they generally are not best for wealthy entrepreneurs because there's little time to keep up with the constant changes in the tax law. The best approach is to seek out an expert who understands the matters that impact entrepreneurs.

Asset Protection

When you become rich and famous, you find that you have lots of friends. Of course, they hope to get a piece of your wealth! This is not to say that you have to distrust everyone you meet. But the fact is that wealthy persons attract unsavory people, so it's important to be cautious.

You should look at something called *asset protection*, which is a way to shield your wealth from potential lawsuits. It's true that the techniques aren't necessarily foolproof—Zuckerberg has been a defendant in many lawsuits—but you should be able to avoid many problems.

Here are some things to consider:

- *Don't sign a personal guarantee:* With this, you are pledging essentially all of your assets to back a potential liability.

- *Have adequate insurance:* You need to periodically inventory your assets, determine their values, and make sure you have enough insurance.

- *Set up protective entities:* These are usually corporations that can own assets. Doing this makes it more difficult for creditors to get access to them. A common entity is a trust. For example, Zuckerberg holds his shares as the trustee of The Mark Zuckerberg 2008 Annuity Trust. He probably structured this for asset protection as well as to get tax benefits.

- *Pay attention to corporate matters:* Read the contracts you sign. Are there areas where you may have personal liability? Your company should also have enough directors and officers insurance. Shareholder lawsuits are common.

Philanthropy

In late 2010, Zuckerberg pledged to donate at least half his wealth to charity. It was part of Bill Gates' "Giving Pledge." Others who have joined include Steve Case, Warren Buffett, Larry Ellison, George Lucas, and Michael Bloomberg.

Zuckerberg has already made donations. The most notable was a $100 million gift to the Newark, NJ, public school system. According to Zuckerberg:

> People wait until late in their career to give back. But why wait when there is so much to be done? With a generation of younger folks who have thrived on the success of their companies, there is a big opportunity for many of us to give back earlier in our lifetime and see the impact of our philanthropic efforts.

It's great advice and shows that money should not be an obsession. It's better to focus on things that matter, which has always been the driving motivation for Zuckerberg. And of all the things covered in this book, that's perhaps the most important lesson to keep in mind.

Conclusion

If I hadn't launched [Facebook] that day, I was about to just can it and go on to the next thing I was about to do.[1]

—Mark Zuckerberg

This book has covered quite a bit. But you shouldn't take everything as gospel. Each company is different, and you must be alert to finding ways to innovate— not only with regard to your product but also the business model and go-to-market strategy.

You need to figure out one major thing: your company needs to solve a difficult problem. Facebook did this by replacing the antiquated ways people kept in contact with each other, including snail-mail, phone, and e-mail. Zuckerberg knew there was a better way.

But he did more than code a web site. He built a platform that focused on the types of relationships that were important to people—and he did this with complex algorithms. He also made the system more robust by allowing third-party developers to create apps for it. In the end, Facebook had tremendous barriers to entry, which made it extremely difficult for competitors to be a threat.

Making this possible was not easy. It took lots of hackathons and sleepless nights. Of course, Zuckerberg had to spend a lot of time recruiting some of the world's best minds. But he understood his mission and how to get there.

This is not to say that you should focus on social networking or the Internet or mobile. True, these areas hold great opportunities for entrepreneurs, but don't get tunnel vision and get sucked into the latest hot area. There are many

[1] Katie Little, "Facebook's Early Days: 'I Was About to Just Can It,'" May 12, 2012, CNBC, www.cnbc.com/id/47378201.

categories to look at when searching for problems to solve. Your impact can perhaps be even more important than Facebook's.

Here are just a few that come to mind.

Computers

Although computers are mostly a commodity, a fortune is waiting to be made by someone who can go beyond the silicon chip. The reason is that within the next 20 years—and probably much sooner—Moore's Law will grind to a halt. Simply put, there will no longer be a doubling of processing power every 18 months. Silicon chips have natural limits in terms of etching transistors, and the technology will become unpredictable due to quantum mechanics.

Without Moore's Law, the computer industry will be in deep trouble. To deal with this, strong research is required into new types of chips, such as those using innovative chemistry or nanotechnology concepts.

Energy

Back in the 1960s, a geophysicist for Shell Oil, Dr. M. King Hubbert, came up with something called the Peak Theory of oil. His contention was that production of oil inevitably reaches maximum levels and then experiences a steep drop.

Hubbert predicted that the US would suffer its peak in oil production in the early 1970s. He came under criticism, but he was eventually proven correct.

His theory points to a peak in Saudi oil in 2007 to 2011 or so. True, he could be wrong on this point. But the fact is that oil prices have remained persistently high over the past decade. At the same time, it's getting tougher to find new deposits.

If the world hits a peak, it could be devastating. Oil is a key driver for wealth.

So for entrepreneurs, this seems like a great opportunity to look at new energy concepts, such as fusion, magnetism, and superconductors. These areas are still in the early stages and should be ripe for tremendous breakthroughs.

Biotechnology

There have been tremendous breakthroughs in this area. The decoding of the genome is incredible.

In 2012, it's possible for you to have a company completely decode your genome for about $1,000. Within ten years, the price tag could drop to $100. If it does, the world will have access to hundreds of millions of genomes that will be key for curing intractable diseases like diabetes, Alzheimer's, cystic fibrosis, HIV, Parkinson's, and cancer. But doing so will require entrepreneurs who have the ability to apply advanced computer systems to biotechnology systems, a process known as *bioinformatics*. This area is definitely worth looking into.

My point is that you need to expand your horizons and go beyond your comfort zone. The next few decades will involve amazing new technologies.

With some helpful tools from this book—and the inspiration of companies like Facebook—it's time for your journey!

Glossary

83(b) Election: Part of the tax code that allows for the immediate vesting of stock. It often results in a lower tax. The election must be made within 30 days of the grant of stock.

Accelerated vesting: When part or all of a person's stock options are vested on the event of a change of control.

Accelerators: Similar to angel groups but may instead have their own office space for the ventures they back. Accelerators tend to provide considerable ongoing advice and mentorship. The top ones include Y Combinator and TechStars.

Accounts receivable: An asset created when a company has sold a product or service but the customer has yet to pay.

Acqui-hire: An acquisition of a company with the main purpose of hiring top engineers. Facebook has made more than 25 such deals.

Angel: A person who invests their own money in early-stage ventures. Such people are usually wealthy and former entrepreneurs.

Anti-dilution clause: Gives existing investors the right to obtain more shares when the next round of funding is at a lower valuation (known as a *down round*).

Asset purchase: An acquisition during which the buyers buy all or most of the seller's assets for stock or cash (or a combination of the two). It helps to avoid liabilities and often has certain tax advantages.

Auditor: A firm that vouches for a company's financial statements. For an IPO, the auditor must be registered with the SEC.

Balance sheet: Financial statement that includes a company's assets, liabilities, and equity. It should always balance according to this equation: Assets = Liabilities + Equity.

Board of directors: A group, ranging from three to ten or so members, that meets every month or so to review progress and weigh in on major decisions. All corporations have them. The board also has the power to appoint and fire the CEO.

Business model: The way a company generates revenues. For Facebook, the primary business model is advertising. But the company also generates substantial revenues from its Payments business.

Capitalization table (also known as the cap table): A list of all the shareholders and their ownership stakes, before and after the proposed financing.

Change of control: Occurs when a company is sold or liquidated. It is a critical event for a person's stock options or equity.

Common stock: The representation of ownership in a company. It usually has some rights, such as voting on important matters.

Conversion right: An investor's right to convert their preferred stock into common stock.

Convertible note: A loan to a company, usually in the early stages. It has a term of anywhere from 6 to 18 months. Once there is a Series A funding, the note is converted into common or preferred stock.

Co-sale agreement: Agreement stating that if a founder sells shares, the rest of the investors have the right to sell a proportionate number of their own shares.

Cost of revenue: Includes all expenses directly related to the delivery of the company's products.

Crowdfunding: Leveraging a public web site to raise funds from the public.

Crowdsourcing: Leveraging a user base to develop something, such as a graphic design.

Daily active user (DAU): A user who visits a site at least one time every day. The DAU is a key driver for Facebook's success.

Data room: A secure online portal where a company can put its due diligence and other investor materials.

Deck: The PowerPoint presentation used for raising capital.

Dividend: A payment from a company to its investors. It can be in the form of cash or stock.

Down round: When the valuation is lower on the next round of funding. Investors try to protect against this with an anti-dilution clause.

Drag-along provision: Requires founders and other key shareholders to vote in favor of a major corporate transaction, such as a sale or merger.

Dual-class structure: When the founder has a special class of stock that grants considerably more voting rights. It is a way to maintain control over the company.

Due diligence: The process of investigating a company's finances and liabilities before an investment is made or an acquisition is completed.

Earnout: Extra cash or stock that employees receive if they hit certain milestones. This is often part of the consideration for an acquisition.

Emerging growth company: Defined in the JOBS Act as a company that has less than $1 billion in revenues. These operators have fewer regulations when coming public.

Engagement: The level of activity for things like wall posts, messages, Likes, comments, and photo uploads.

Freemium model: When a company has a fully functional free version of its product. The goal is to convert a small part of the user base—say, 1% to 5%—to adopt a premium version. The free product is essentially a form of marketing.

GAAP (Generally Accepted Accounting Principles): An extensive set of accounting principles that have been developed by authorities such as the Securities and Exchange Commission, the American Institute of Certified Public Accountants (AICPA), the Financial Accounting Standards Board (FASB), and the Public Company Accounting Oversight Board (PCAOB).

Goodwill: The value from an acquisition. It is the purchase price minus the net asset value of the target company.

Gross profit: Revenues minus the cost of revenue.

Gross profit margin: Gross profit divided by sales.

Hackathon: A contest for coders to create an app in a short period of time, such as over the weekend. It's something Facebook created to improve creativity.

Hold-back: Money set aside in an escrow in case of any breaches of representations and warranties from an acquisition.

Income statement: Financial statement that starts with revenues and then subtracts all costs. The result is either a profit or a loss.

Indemnification: Guarantee that a corporation will cover the liabilities of investors and the board, such as in the event of a shareholder lawsuit.

Information rights: An investor's right to inspect a company's books.

Invention assignment: Transfer of all intellectual property created by an employee to the employer.

Investment bank: A firm that provides advisory services for mergers and acquisitions and IPOs.

IPO (Initial Public Offering): The first time a company issues stock to the public.

JOBS Act: Legislation passed in 2012 to make it easier for smaller companies to raise capital and come public. One of the areas it legalized is crowdfunding.

Late-stage funder: An investor such as a private equity fund, hedge fund, or mutual fund that invests in a company when it becomes large enough. Often, the money is used to buy shares from existing investors and employees; this is known as a secondary purchase.

Letter of intent (LOI): The first offer to buy another company. It sets the main terms, such as the valuation, the type of consideration, and the legal protections.

Liquidation preference: Gives priority to the investor when there is a liquidity event, such as an acquisition. The most basic is a 1X preference. This means the investor gets back up to 1 times the investment before anyone else receives any cash.

Market capitalization (or market cap): The stock price times the number of shares outstanding. It shows the overall value of a company.

Noncompete clause: Agreement that forbids a person to compete against a former employer or client, usually for a period of time. In some states, including California, such clauses generally are not enforceable because they prevent people from pursing employment opportunities. However, if a noncompete is part of an acquisition, it is usually enforceable.

Nondisclosure agreement (NDA): A legal agreement that forbids a party from disclosing certain information, usually for a period of time. Such agreements are generally enforceable.

Nonsolitication: Agreement that says you are not allowed to poach customers or suppliers from your former employer. Interestingly, California looks unfavorably on these types of arrangements.

No-shop clause: Agreement that says a company may not seek out an alternative deal when there is a proposed funding or acquisition.

Option pool: The percentage of total options available to grant to employees. It is usually 5% to 20% of the outstanding stock.

Pay-to-play provision: Encourages existing investors to participate in the next round of funding by requiring them to convert their shares to common stock if they don't participate.

Post-money valuation: The valuation of a company after an investment is made. It is equal to the pre-money valuation plus the total amount of the financing round.

Preferred stock: Representation of ownership in a company, with special rights and protections such as liquidation preferences, veto rights, and board seats.

Pre-money valuation: The valuation of a company before outside investment.

Protective provisions: Veto rights for investors. They cover areas such as the sale of the company, amendments to the certificate of incorporation, and issuances of new securities.

Redemption right: An investor's right to get their money back after a fixed period of time.

Registration rights: The rights of investors when there is a filing of an IPO.

Representations and warranties: Promises made by a company that is in the process of being sold. If there are any breaches, the buyer has the right to seek damages.

Resale restriction (also known as a right of first refusal or ROFR): The right of a company to buy back shares at the current valuation or select its own buyer.

Restricted stock: Stock that a company grants to an employee but that is subject to vesting. When the vesting requirements are earned, the employee has ownership rights to the stock.

Road show: The presentations that senior management makes to investors a couple of weeks before an IPO.

S-1: The document filed with the Securities and Exchange Commission to go public. It includes the prospectus, which is the key document that sets forth a company's business plan, financials, and risk factors.

Sarbanes-Oxley Act (SOX): A law passed in 2002 to prevent accounting scandals. It introduced higher disclosure requirements and increased criminal penalties.

Secondary market: An online exchange that allows investors and employees of a private company to sell their shares. The two main operators are SharesPost and SecondMarket.

Glossary

Securities and Exchange Commission (SEC): The federal agency that enforces securities laws, such as for IPOs and private fundings.

Seed funding: A company's first financing from outside investors.

Series A: The first round of financing when institutional investors participate, such as venture capitalists.

Social context: Advertising that is based on engaging friends based on activities such as Liking an advertiser's Facebook page. The idea is that people will probably value a friend's recommendations more than a straight ad.

Sponsored stories: Ads than let an advertiser broadcast messages to more of its fans.

Stealth startup: A company that remains secret as it develops its product.

Stock option: An employee's right to buy a fixed number of shares at a certain price. The employee must stay with the company for a period of time to have the right to exercise the option; this is known as vesting.

Stock purchase: Acquisition during which the buyer purchases all or a majority of the shares from the seller. It tends to be favorable to the seller.

Strategic investor: A large company that invests in early-stage companies.

Super angel: A high-profile person who invests in early-stage ventures. Such investors usually invest substantial amounts, such as over $1 million. They may also invest other people's money.

Term sheet: The offer of funding from an angel or VC. It is a few pages long and sets forth the key terms, such as the valuation, amount, and protections.

Underwriter: A Wall Street firm that manages the IPO process.

Venture lender: A financial firm that provides loans to early-stage companies. The terms are usually 6 to 18 months.

Vesting: The process of earning the right to buy shares of a stock option. This usually means an employee must continue to work for a company for a set period of time. A typical vesting schedule is for a one-year cliff and then three years of monthly vesting. That is, after one year, the employee has the right to buy 25% of the shares of the option. After this, an incremental amount of shares vest each month.

Virtual good: A digital item that a person can buy. Often, this is for a social game, such as from Zynga. Facebook has a Payments platform to allow for these transactions.

Warrant: Similar to an option, which gives the right to buy a fixed number of shares for a certain price. There is no vesting. A warrant is usually granted as part of a funding.

Work for hire: A clause often found in a contractor's agreement. It means the clients own all the intellectual property.

Index

Printed in Great Britain
by Amazon

58934897R00120